Aunt Jane's
HERO

Calvary Press
PUBLISHING
PO Box 805
Amityville, NY 11701
1-800-789-8175
www.calvarypress.com

Aunt Jane's
HERO

Elizabeth Prentiss

Calvary Press Publishing
P.O. Box 805
Amityville, NY 11701
U.S.A.
1-(800)-789-8175

ISBN 1-879737-34-5

Calvary Press can be found on the World Wide Web at:
calvarypress.com

Cover Design by Anthony Rotolo

Prentiss, Elizabeth, 1818-1878
    Stepping Heavenward
Recommended Dewey Decimal Classification: 234
Suggested Subject Headings:
1. Fiction—Christian—Family
2. Religion—Christian literature—Christian Home
3. Christian literature—Devotional—Elizabeth Prentiss
I. Title

Manufactured in the United States of America
1 2 3 4 5 6 7 8 9 10   99 00 01 02

Foreword
by Susan Hunt

I love this book! It is a marriage manual of the highest order—a biblical perspective of the Christian home and a call to women to be the helpers God designed us to be, all rolled into one. It's a must-read for every married woman and ought to be required reading for every bride-to-be.

Aunt Jane's Hero is delightful reading. Elizabeth Prentiss skillfully draws us into this lovely story, but she doesn't stop there. She gently weaves elements into the story that bring us face-to-face with woman's potential for good or harm in a marriage. Her love for Jesus and her passion for homes that reflect His grace and mercy spill over onto every page.

Every woman needs an Aunt Jane, and through her books, Elizabeth Prentiss becomes Aunt Jane for us all. Her godly wisdom and her charming wit transcend time and place. She is the quintessential Titus 2 woman.

Whether you are at the beginning or well along the way in your marriage journey, *Aunt Jane's Hero* will encourage you. Married or not, this book will equip you to be an Aunt Jane to other women.

Aunt Jane's Hero is a book you'll want to read over and over again, and each time, you'll find new encouragement and a deeper understanding of the godly home.

Atlanta, Georgia
November 16, 1998

THEY were living to themselves: self, with its hopes, and promises, and dreams, still had hold of them; but the Lord began to fulfill their prayers. They had asked for contrition, and He sent them sorrow; they had asked for purity, and He sent them thrilling anguish; they had asked to be meek, and He had broken their hearts; they had asked to be dead to the world, and he slew all their living hopes; they had asked to be made like unto Him, and He placed them in the furnace, sitting by "as a refiner of silver," till they should reflect His image; they had asked to lay hold of His cross, and when He had reached it to them, it lacerated their hands. They had asked they knew not what, nor how; but He had taken them at their word, and granted them all their petitions. They were hardly willing to follow on so far, or to draw so nigh to Him. They had upon them an awe and fear, as Jacob at Bethel, or Eliphaz in the night visions, or as the apostles when they thought they had seen a spirit, and knew not that it was Jesus. They could almost pray Him to depart from them, or to hide his awfulness. They found it easier to obey than to suffer—to do than to give up—to bear the cross than to hang upon it: but they cannot go back, for they have come too near the unseen cross, and its virtues have pierced too deeply within them. He is fulfilling to them his promise, "And I, if I be lifted up, will draw all men unto me."

"But now, at last, their turn is come. Before, they had only heard of the mystery, but now they feel it. He has fastened on them His look of love, as He did on Mary and Peter, and they cannot but choose to follow. Little by little, from time to time, by flitting gleams the mystery of His cross shines upon them. They behold Him lifted up—they gaze on the glory which rays forth from the wounds of His holy passion; and as they gaze, they advance, and are changed into His likeness, and His name shines out through them, for he dwells in them. They live alone with Him above, in unspeakable fellowship; willing to lack what others own, and to be unlike all, so that they are only like him.

"Such are they in all ages who follow the Lamb

*whithersoever He goeth. Had they chosen for them-
selves, or their friends chosen for them, they would
have chosen otherwise. They would have been brighter
here, but less glorious in His kingdom. They would
have had Lot's portion, not Abraham's. If they had
halted anywhere—if He had taken off His hand, and
let them stray back—what would they not have lost?
What forfeits in the morning of the resurrection? But
He stayed them up, even against themselves. Many a
time their foot had well-nigh slipped; but He, in
mercy, held them up; now, even in this life, they know
all he did was done well. It was good for them to
suffer* here, *for they shall reign* hereafter—*to bear the
cross* below, *for they shall wear the crown* above; *and
that not* their *will but* His *was done on them.*"

AUNT JANE'S HERO.

CHAPTER I.

"WELL, Horace!"

"Well, Aunt Jane!"

"I thought you were dead and buried!"

"And I hoped you were!"

"On the whole, I am glad you are alive and well, for I am finishing off a piece of work in the greatest haste possible, and want somebody to thread my needles."

"I sha'n't thread a single one; I want you to talk, and you can't talk when you are at work. Besides, I came to get rested, and it tires me to see you sewing. Why will women always persist in going about armed with work-baskets?"

"Why will men persist in wearing out their clothes? Come take this seat and give an account of yourself."

The speakers were a little old lady, with bright

eyes, and a tall young man with a pair of good humored blue ones. She was not really his aunt, but only an intimate friend, who chose to be called "Aunt Jane," and so Aunt Jane she was.

Horace seated himself, and neither spoke for several minutes. At last he said:

"Upon my word, you are treating me very shabbily, Aunt Jane. I have come all the way up here in this terrible storm to hear you talk, and there you sit, as silent as the grave."

"I really think that among all the people I know you are the greatest hypocrite," was the reply. "You came because you knew that you should probably find me at home this stormy night, and should get a good chance to talk yourself."

Horace laughed.

"Very well. Since you have the faculty of reading a man's motives, suppose you go on and read out my thoughts for me. What did I come to say?"

"Something ridiculous, no doubt, or you would have unburdened yourself sooner."

"You are too bad, Aunt Jane. If I had not given my solemn promise to tell you all about it, I would not utter another word. However, to be out with it once for all—I'm in love!"

"Pshaw; you know better."

"Indeed, I did not do it on purpose," pursued

the young man. "But I met with such a glorious creature"—

"I hate glorious creatures!"

"But I admire them. Just let me tell you"—

"First of all tell me one thing. Is this glorious creature in love with you?"

"Why no, not exactly. That is to say, I've never asked her. But she treats me with great consid eration."

"I should hope so."

"Aunt Jane, if you hadn't such a knack at making a fellow love and admire you, I should almost hate you."

"I thought glorious creatures were your ideal, and I am not glorious, by any means. My dear boy, if I supposed you were really in earnest in this thing, that your heart was really touched by it, I could become tenderly and motherly in an instant. You know that."

"Yes, I do," he said, catching warmly in both his, the hand she held out to him. "Well, I am in earnest; I am fairly caught at last."

"I am very sorry to hear it," she said, seriously. "For of course you cannot afford to marry this young lady."

"No, nor any young lady," he returned, gloomily.

"Don't be vexed with me if I deny that. It is

1*

true that you cannot afford to take a glorious creature to wife; but why not content yourself with
one that isn't glorious: a dear little bit of flesh and
blood, who would not be above keeping your ac-
counts, mending your stockings and the like?
You needn't shake your head."

"I am not shaking it. But you seem to have
forgotten that our last quarrel was on this very
point. You upbraided me for not marrying, and I
told you I couldn't afford it."

"Our last quarrel," she said, musingly,—"we've
had so many that I really don't remember where
it ranks. But I should have said that our last little
tiff was on the subject of cigars."

"They came in for their share of abuse, as they
always do," he returned.

"Well, to go back to your new flame"—

"My first flame, you mean."

"I mean just what I say. Who talked to me of
Anna Perrit by the hour together? Who"—

"That was the merest fancy. Of course, I don't
deny my fancies. All young men have them."

"And who carried a photograph of Grace Harrod
in his pocket for six months; a stolen one at that?"

"It was a mean thing to rob your album, Aunt
Jane, but she was such a pretty creature, and"—

"And such a flirt; yes, I remember; and then
there was that affair with Juliet Moore"—

"Really, Aunt Jane, you have the most inconvenient memory!" cried Horace, moving uncomfortably in his chair. "To hear you talk, one would fancy me a most fickle as well as a most susceptible youth. What is a man to do? Is he to associate with old ladies only? I don't know a fellow who gallants girls about as little as I do. But if you had no home but a boarding-house, and were welcomed by half a dozen pleasant families, I have no doubt you would spend some of your evenings in a little harmless chat with the young ladies there."

"If you would once come out, fair and square, and own that you are a regular flirt, quite as accomplished in that line as any girl of our acquaintance, I could get on with you. But you beat about the bush, and skulk behind trees, so that one never gets a fair shot at you."

"I don't know about the fair shots, but I do know I've received a good many unfair ones. As to yourself, you never lose a chance. I am sorry that I have owned up about Miss"—

"Well, Miss who?"

"I can't tell her name."

"Then you'll break your solemn promise. But that won't surprise me."

"You'll only laugh at me when I tell you who it is. Do you know Mr. Fitzsimmons of the Fifth Avenue?"

"Now, Horace Wheeler, you don't pretend to say that you are carried away with that hollow, heartless creature!"

"With Mr. Fitzsimmons? No, not exactly."

"Don't joke about so serious a matter. So, it is Miss Shoddy, after all, to whom you have given your heart!"

"I wish I hated you, Aunt Jane! I came to get a motherly word of counsel, or of sympathy at least, and you do nothing but mock me. Good night; I'm off."

"You dear, foolish boy, you shall do no such thing!" she cried. "You hav'n't in all the world a better friend than I am. I love you as if you were my own, my very own son. Sit down and let us talk this over."

Yes, she did love him, and he knew it. She had befriended him when he came to this great city years before; had opened her home and heart to him; had scolded, petted, laughed at, borne with him as no one else had done since his mother, her dearest friend, had left him alone in the world. And though, in some moods, she provoked him, and hunted all his little bad habits unto death, he loved her with almost filial affection.

"You women are all alike," he said, subsiding into his seat again. "You banter, and hector, and badger us till we are angry with you, and then

you magically entice us back into your hearts. I
don't know how you do it; I wish I did."

"I can tell you how we do it," she said, earnestly. "It is by being genuine. There is no art or
trickery in a true woman. She will not flatter, she
will not stoop to humor pet vices, but fighting
and conquering them she will give her whole loving heart to him she has thus blessed."

Horace looked into the face now full of expres-
sion and of feeling, with almost boyish admiration.

"If you always looked and talked as you do
now," he said, "you would spoil me for the ordinary run of girls. I should form a new ideal, and
marry not till I found her."

"You would get tired of me if I were always on
stilts," she said, smilingly. "Why should not a
woman be like nature, sometimes spring, sometimes autumn, now summer, now winter? But,
Horace, I must once more repeat, at the risk of
offending and repelling you, that you are on the
wrong track. You are trying to live in the world,
mingling in all its gayeties and follies, and expecting a great deal from it, but doing nothing to make
it wiser or better. You have worked your way
into what you call good society, but that has made
a great gulf between yourself and Christian society. Now just answer this one question; How
many really warm friends have you in this city?"

"Why, as to that, I do not know that I have any. But the people with whom I associate are well-bred, agreeable and refined. And really, Aunt Jane, you can't expect a young man situated as I am, to be as strict as you are. I think one can be good without turning one's back upon the world."

"May I ask you one more question, Horace? Are you living a life of prayer amid all the distractions of the times?"

"That is a question you have no right to ask," he said, coloring.

"Perhaps it is," she said, gently. "There was a time in my history when I should have resented such a question; yet it was a time when it would have been well for my soul had some loving voice asked it. The thought of your throwing yourself away on a mere worldly, fashionable young lady; you who are so formed for a sweet Christian home, makes me shudder."

"I can't imagine how you keep up your interest in me, while we differ so on what you consider vital points."

"I will tell you," she said. "Had my boy lived he would be just your age, and I have associated you with his memory. And just as my prayers would have pulled him out of a dangerous path, so I believe they will pull you."

"It must be comfortable to have such faith in one's own prayers," he said, thoughtlessly.

Her eyes filled with tears.

"It is not faith in my prayers, but faith in Him who dictates them," she said. "Dear Horace, don't stay away so long again; bear with my little sermons for the sake of my love to you."

"I will," he said, "but you will never make me feel as you do."

CHAPTER II.

HORACE WHEELER was a young man of fair abilities and some culture. He was handsome and quick-witted, and wide-awake; a favorite everywhere, because of his unfailing good humor and the comfortable sense of his own powers of pleasing, which made him self-possessed and easy under all circumstances. He was not more susceptible than the ordinary run of men of his age, but still contrived to have always on hand something bordering on a love affair. In fact, "the girls" did all they could to spoil him, and he would have been spoiled but for Aunt Jane, who kept a sharp eye upon him, and often painted his portrait for him in anything but flattering colors. And now Georgiana Fitzsimmons had him in tow, and was sailing off with him, as well as with half-a-dozen other bewildered victims. He admired her royal beauty, her style, her faultless mode of dress, and it was a luxury to spend an evening with her in the richly furnished

parlors which offered such a contrast to his own
poor quarters. She played and sang well, and was
never at a loss for something to say; it did not occur to him that this endless flow of small talk was
very small indeed, nor did it once strike him that
her papa and mamma, whose house this was, did
not dare to show their plebeian faces in their own
parlors. Miss Georgiana's idea of a father was of
a man who spent his life in making money for her
to spend—of a mother, as a woman who looked
after the servants, ordered good dinners, and kept
out of her way on all desirable occasions. To be
sure, papa Fitzsimmons sometimes grumbled at
the way in which money went, and declared that
he was a poor man, and that mamma Fitzsimmons
often wept, maintaining that nobody had such ungrateful children as hers. But these little speeches
rippled lightly over their gay daughter's heart, allowing that she had one, and never for one moment, disturbed her peace of mind. She found it
quite agreeable to have lovers; it was out of the
question to go into society with such a figure of a
man as papa, who, as she often assured him, only
knew enough to sell calico, and it was convenient to have fine-looking young men like Horace
Wheeler attend her when she went out. And it is
amazing how, under a guise of sweet simplicity
and unconsciousness, some girls can conceal an

artifice that would do credit to a veteran. Each
of the young men in her train fancied himself the
favored one; if one of these poor wretches gave
signs of escaping her clutches, as they sometimes
did, (for she took a cat-like pleasure in letting her
mice run for the fun of catching them again,) she
had a sweet word, a captivating smile equal to the
emergency. She meant to get married to somebody, but not now; she wanted to have what she
called "a good time" with a dozen or two young
men first; meaning by a good time, though she
never quite owned that to herself, the being a little
in love with each and all in turn, and having them
each and all in love with her. And when they
severally reached that point they ceased to interest
her, and she turned to new ones. And this was
the "glorious creature" who had caught Horace;
she had let him run three or four times, overtaken
and patted and bewildered and made him her cap-
tive again, and was finding this a pastime of peculiar pleasure.

"How long it is since you were here!" with a
reproachful, charming look. "I began to think
you were getting tired of me!"

Or, "I saw you at the last rehearsal, and you
never gave me so much as a glance."

"Ah, you saw me then!" with a gratified throb
of the real heart he kept under his waistcoat.

"How very strange! for I kept behind a pillar all the evening. I had the blues, and did not want to be seen."

"Really? But you should always come to me when you are low-spirited, I feel so much for my friends, and you are such an old friend!"

And this old friend of six months would have liked to prove to her, on the spot, what a friend he was. But there was Joe Fisher watching them both, trying to carry on an animated conversation with the lady on his arm, yet to hear every word spoken by these twain.

He must bide his time, but he was making up his mind that in spite of Aunt Jane, he must, at least, become engaged to his heroine. They were both young, and need not think of marriage yet; Will Jones had confidentially revealed to him that the three years of his own engagement had been delightful ones, and that Adela, his wife, was not half so nice now that they had settled down together.

"She used to say," moaned Will, "that she adored the smell of a cigar, and now she says it makes her sick. And she often spoke of my auburn hair as so much to her taste, but now she calls it red."

"And no wonder," thought Horace, and hugged himself for joy that his Georgiana was one of the sort to wear well; as unlike Mrs. Jones as possible. He neglected all his friends now; some wondered what had become of him, some secretly smiled at his infatuation; one almost rejoiced in it; Aunt Jane knew just how the whole thing would end, and felt that it would not hurt him to have a little of the wind taken out of his sails. He had assumed the attitude of a man who had only to choose what flower to pick, and this not merely because he was so steeped in natural self-conceit, but from the fact that he had been flattered and caressed into it. And this conceit was not becoming to him in her eyes.

Horace had never laid anything but flowers on the shrine of his beloved, but he now thought it time to offer her some gift that should at once prove his admiration and his refined, cultivated taste. What should it be? He tried to lie awake nights to think about it, but unfortunately his perfect health forbade that, and he never knew what happened after he laid his head on his pillow until he awoke next morning. At last he bethought him of a ring of some value, that had been his mother's. He could put this ring upon her finger, and at the same time whisper some words that would reveal that to one human being only could he entrust this sacred relic. Georgiana would shed tears, half accept and half refuse it; he should then

in this tender moment speak of his hopeless love—
hopeless, because of his poverty and her position,
and she should throw herself into his arms, declaring that a cottage with him, etc., etc.

He went over this little programme a good many
times before there was the least chance of carrying
it out. Georgiana was so sweetly unconscious
that he was dying for a chance to see her alone;
she knew so little what she was in herself and what
she was to him, and let such very inferior young
men hang around her.

This unconscious creature was really communing
with herself after this wise.

"I may as well let him propose; he comes so
often now that people are beginning to talk. And
all the rest are hanging back, thinking I like him.
And of course I do like him. He's so handsome
and dotes on me so; but then I've always let him
see that I did not care particularly for him, at least
he might see it if he would, but men are so conceited."

And so it *happened*, one evening, that on being
ushered into the parlor where he had spent so
many agreeable hours, Horace found Miss Georgiana quite alone, and began to put his little plan
into execution. He had a sufficiently good opinion of himself to be in general quite self-possessed,
but now that the long-coveted hour had arrived,

he felt sheepish and wished the thing well over.
She sat before him provokingly pretty and provokingly cool, her hands folded lightly together in her
lap, and somehow he got possession of one of them,
and slipped his dead mother's ring upon a finger.

"What queer, old-fashioned thing have you
picked up, Mr. Wheeler?" she asked, gazing at it
through her eye-glass. "Dear me, I never saw
anything so very peculiar; indeed you must not
ask me to wear it; it would set people talking,
you know."

"It was my mother's wedding-ring," he stam-
mered, "and I hoped that for her sake, for my
sake"—

She laughed merrily and musically, and knew
that she did.

"But you know, Mr. Wheeler, I never saw your
mother, and couldn't be expected—really," as the
poor fellow blundered on, "you surprise me greatly.
You must see that I am fancy free, that I have no
preference for any gentleman."

"But you have looked, you have acted, you have
said"—

"I hope you do not intend to insinuate that I
have given you any encouragement, Mr. Wheeler."

"No," he said, a little angrily, for her self-pos-
session and suavity unnerved him, "I never deal
in insinuations. What I have to say I say plainly,

and in so many words. And I say you have led
me into this ridiculous, mortifying position by a
long series of deliberate and heartless acts."

"I could not have believed you were so unchar-
itable," she returned, smiling. "It is very disagreeable, but I forgive you, and we will be as
good friends as ever; shall we not?" She held
out her hand, as she spoke, but he did not take it.

"Heaven have mercy on the man that wins it!"
he said, and bowed himself majestically out.

For once in her life she felt uncomfortable, and
she had a whole evening in which to face herself,
for, expecting a long interview with Horace, she
had given orders that no one else should be ad-
mitted.

"I never gave him the least encouragement, not
the very least," she said to herself. "And how
could he suppose that *I* should *look* at him? A
poor lawyer, whose wife would have to sweep her
own parlors, provided she had any, which I do not
suppose she would. However, I can't help it if
men will make fools of themselves. I must tell
Harriet Foot about it; how she will laugh!"

This thought quite restored her spirits; she sent
a servant to summon Harriet, who lived next door,
and gave her a magnified picture of the whole
scene, and the twain made themselves merry over
the rejected lover, eating chocolate caramels the

while, in an insatiable way, quite after the manner of girls in general.

Now we do not intend to insinuate that all young ladies, in what is called "good society," are thoughtless and heartless; but that this is a hot-bed in which they are likely to thrive. Who goes home from a ball, to kneel down and pray to God? Who leaves the theatre with new longings after eternal life? Who pretends that going to the opera prepares one for hard, self-denying, Christian work?

Would that some eloquent hand could paint the contrast between Miss Fitzsimmons and what she had refused to give to Horace, and what one earnest, Christian heart, unseen by all the world, was at that moment giving him! For while the one laughed, the other prayed; and those prayers were so many guardian angels that prevented, encompassed—saved him.

CHAPTER III.

ORACE WHEELER had stood up years before, in the little village church, and confessed Christ before men. He was then not much more than a boy, and had very indefinite notions as to what this step implied and involved. Indeed, he had been urged into it by his mother, whose delicate health made it probable that she would not live to see him safely through the perils of early youth, and who felt that she could die in peace if she could leave him in the sheltering bosom of the church she loved. She died soon after he entered college, and so he lost the letters that would have counselled and stimulated and blessed him. Shall we say he lost her prayers, also? God only knows. His father, a grave, hard, good man, prayed for, but rarely wrote to him; he had never had either sister or brother.

Perhaps all this made old Mrs. Faulkner peculiarly dear to him, when on his establishing himself in this great city, she became to him almost a mother. But all he knew of religion was what his own meagre experience had taught him, and all he knew of young women he had learned in society. And he had, so far, got very little comfort out of either. So now when he marched smarting and stinging out of Miss Fitzsimmons' ceiled house, he never once thought of such a thing as making the pain she had cost him a religious discipline; nor did he fly to the genial presence of other ladies in the hope of finding solace in their society. On the contrary, he fell to generalizing in this style:

"They're all alike, and I knew it, and yet have been and made a fool of myself. All they care for or think of, is dress and show and fashion. There isn't enough heart in the whole concern to make one warm, manly heart. If you can put diamond rings on their fingers, and give them palaces to live in, and let them drive about in carriages, they may condescend to let you sit at the same table, and escort them whithersoever they would go. But offer them your unknown name, and your faithful, honest heart, and they'll laugh in your face!

"To think how they'll get their heads together and discuss me, and giggle and cackle as only girls and geese can! I can see that simpering Harriet Foot, Georgiana's crony and toady, swallowing the whole story, and then running to tell *her* crony."

He went back to his room, lighted it, pulled off his boots and tossed them spitefully against the wall, jerked on his slippers, and flung himself into a chair. If he had had a fire to poke at, that would have been of some consolation; he could have knocked the coals out of the grate and picked them up with the tongs, and fancied each of them to be Georgiana Fitzsimmons as he did so. But the room was warmed by hot pipes, and offered him no employment, no relief to his troubled thoughts. He believed himself to be a very wretched, much abused man, mistaking the storm of passion that swept across his soul, and the bitter mortification under which he suffered, for the pangs of a broken, disappointed heart.

Much abused he certainly was, but not so very wretched, for a cigar quite soothed and comforted him, and he went to bed in due time, and slept better than Georgiana did, after all the sweet things she had been eating.

And while he was dressing he began to congratulate himself that he had got off so well, though he still twinged at the remembrance of the way in which a girl five years younger than himself had shown her superiority in worldly wisdom.

When he reached his office he found a note from

Aunt Jane awaiting him, in which she asked him to drop in "accidentally" that evening. He thought he might as well go and get laughed at, and have it over with, and sent an amusing reply, in which he promised to do all sorts of accidental things, adding that Miss Fitzsimmons had given him the mitten, and that it was a very warm mitten indeed, and that now he should never marry unless Aunt Jane herself would take pity on him.

At eight o'clock he was ushered into her home-like domains, and found himself, to his great disgust, at a sewing circle. He had got himself up quite nicely, considering how wretched he was, and looked very handsome and attractive as he made his way through a little crowd of girls, busy in dressing dolls. They had already dressed thirty-two, who stood in rows on the piano, leaning against each other for support, and looking like sixteen pairs of twins; and were engaged on as many more. Several young men lounged about the room, pretending to help, and making all sorts of absurd remarks, which the maidens deemed very witty. After speaking to Aunt Jane, Horace took a seat among the rest, and fell into a bantering talk with those near him, while he cynically looked at this array of pretty, fresh girls, whom, in his heart, he regarded as so many embryo flirts. A little creature sat apart from the rest, who, he was sure, had not yet left school; she was at work upon a crying-baby, which she was getting into long clothes. He would not have given her a look or a thought, for she sat with her back to him and was quite absorbed in her task, but that she faced a mirror, which faithfully reflected her. It amused him to watch her thus off her guard, with a sweet, matronly look gradually stealing over her almost childish face as the baby became every moment more life-like in her hands. At last she had given it a final touch, and secure from observation as she fancied herself, went into rapture over this pretty mockery of a human child, kissing, fondling and playing with it just as a young mother caresses and sports with her baby of flesh and blood—her baby with a soul.

"The little thing has got a heart of her own," mused Horace, looking curiously on, "but she won't have one long. It will be cooled out of her as soon as she goes into that charming sphere called society." His lip curled at the thought, and at that moment she looked up and saw that he had been observing and was despising her. He saw her face crimson painfully, knew that she had misunderstood the contempt of his glance, and was shocked at himself for his carelessness. But he did a right-minded manly thing, which was just like him, when he rose and made his way to her and said, frankly and warmly:

"I played the spy, it is true, but I did not dream

that I sat in such a position that there was the least
chance of detection."

"If people will do silly, childish things they must
expect to be laughed at," she said.

"But I was not laughing at you," said Horace;
"I was admiring you with all my might."

"That is a very likely story," she said, a little
comforted, and a good deal re-assured by his manner, but she went off with her baby, leaving him
ready to burst with repressed amusement, for all
the time they had stood talking together, she had
been pressing its little round, unconscious cheek
against her own hardly less round. His instinct
told him not to follow her, and he said to himself
besides, that she was not much more than a child,
and so he tried to make himself agreeable to those
who were older.

This was a different set of girls from that in
which he had been idling for two or three years.
Each of them lived for a purpose; perhaps not
quite consciously, certainly not very grandly; but
their Sunday work in a mission-school had given
them a degree of elevation above mere triflers.
They were in great glee this evening, for they
were getting ready for a Christmas festival, and
the doll-dressing being now over, Aunt Jane ushered them into the dining-room, where, seated at a
long table, they were to fill cornucopias with sugar-

plums. And the broken-hearted Horace caught the spirit of the little company, and enjoyed the innocent mirth of these unspoiled girls; a man who could afford to get married might be happy with almost any of them he said to himself, but, of course, he was not that man. Though he had tucked a cottage into the programme in which Georgiana was to figure, he had never thought of such a thing as living in one; it wasn't the style, now-a-days, and a brown stone house was more to his taste.

When the company broke up, and while the girls were getting into their sacks and hats, he had a few moments with Aunt Jane, who, to his great relief, made no allusion to his discomfited condition, but thanked him for coming, and asked him to see one or more of her young friends safely home. Observing his little heroine of the baby scene standing near, he offered her his services as an escort,

"No, I am not going anywhere," she said; "I am making Aunt Jane a visit."

"Aunt Jane!" he repeated, "then you and I are cousins."

"Indeed we are not, for she is not really my aunt; I only call her so because I love her so, and because she lets me."

"That makes our relationship doubly near," he

said, laughingly, "for she is not my aunt, either; I
call her so because I love her so, and because she
lets me."

He repeated her words and her manner of speaking them so perfectly, that she thought, as before,
that he was secretly laughing at her; but she looked up and said, gently:

"We country girls come to the city expecting
to say and do foolish things, and get laughed at for
our pains."

"But why will you persist in fancying that I am
laughing at you, my dear little *cousin?*" he cried,
and he was going on to add, patronizingly, "on
the contrary I really like you," when his eye wandered from her sweet upturned face to her two
little plump hands, and he saw that they were as
red as they were plump.

"She's nothing but a stupid little country girl,
after all," he said to himself, "though where she
picked up such lady-like manners, it would be hard
to guess;" so then he took himself off and thought
of her no more.

But she thought of him a good many times,
wondered who he was, hoped he would come
again, knew three minutes after she got to church
or into any public place whether he was there,
and was always expecting to meet him on the
street when she walked out. In spite of all which,

she had a charming visit at Aunt Jane's, and went home at the end of three weeks, where she was nearly eaten up by those who were glad to get her and her useful hands back again, even though they were red.

Well, Horace Wheeler, you made a great mistake when you let her slip out of your hands. This sweet, loving, Christian girl would have aroused the feeble Christian life now almost dead in your soul, and made a home for you of which any man might be proud. And so Aunt Jane would have said if she had had a chance, but he did not give her one. He kept away from her week after week; her little sermons, as he called them, were of all things most repugnant to him. He had been drinking at broken fountains, but felt sure that the world had some full ones which sooner or later would quench his thirst.

2*

CHAPTER IV.

THE season this year was unusually gay, and Horace plunged into it headlong. Everybody wanted him at their dancing parties, their private theatricals, their musical festivals; his tall, graceful figure was an ornament, and his gay sallies passed for keenest wit. He had to meet Georgiana repeatedly, but his air of lofty indifference kept her at a distance, while it secretly vexed her, for she had, thus far, found no one to take his place. But he went home from these gay scenes out of spirits, and in spite of himself had his hours of reflection, when there came to him uncomfortable intimations that he was not living the true life for which he was born.

"Well," he would reply, "if a man lives in the world he must be of it. Some may spend their time in driving Mission-schools and Sunday-schools, and all that sort of thing, but we can't all be doing it, any more than we can all be ministers

and fall to preaching. I am as strict as most young
fellows; father doesn't think so, it is true, but the
world has got ahead of him, and has none of his
old-fashioned ways. It does not hurt me to go to
the theatre, or to dance, or to play a harmless game
of cards; in fact I feel that I ought to take my own
independent course in such matters. I am as regular at church as any of them; if I don't go to
prayer-meetings it is because there are so few
evenings in the week, and because I do not enjoy
them. And as to taking a class in a Mission-school,
as Aunt Jane is always saying I ought, why, I
should have to get up an hour earlier than I do
usually, and it is bad enough as it is. And at any
rate I can't do it just now, for it would set everybody to talking and saying how my trials had been
blessed to me; and that I couldn't stand."

Now there was a man of a sorrowful countenance and of a sorrowful spirit away off in a little
country-town, praying for his only son at these
very moments, and his prayers were going to pre-
vail. The knowledge that his boy, his dead wife's
boy, was living a worldly, useless life, in defiance
of the training he had had, and the vows he had
taken upon himself, had crushed out what little
gladness he ever had in him, and that was not
much. He believed that Horace was really regen-
erate, and that his soul would be saved at last;

but that did not give him much, if it did any, relief, when he set it off against the awful fact that
he was not, in any sense, living for the glory of
God, but simply to and for himself. And ever and
anon when he was pleading for his son with strong
crying and tears, there would surge up in the soul
of that son unwelcome, painful thoughts; recollections of his mother and his mother's teachings,
faint yearnings for a faith and a practice like hers.
He wist not whence they came, nor what a fearful
risk he ran when he resisted and stifled them.

It was Sunday, and, as usual, when he went to
church regularly anywhere, he sat with Aunt Jane
in her pew. He had a bad habit of wandering
about from church to church, with no special preference for any one, and she had not seen him at
hers for some weeks. He behaved himself now with
great outward devotion; took off his glove rever-
ently, as his mother had taught him to do, as he sat
at the sacramental table and received the sacred
bread and wine, and joined in the hymns with apparent fervor. Aunt Jane's heart yearned for him;
how much this festival meant to her—how little to
him! And as she silently prayed for him, he felt
the old discomfort creeping over him, the sense of
unrest experienced, at times, at least, by every human soul that tries to satisfy its infinite longings
and yearnings with finite things. "Will you come

home with me to tea?" she whispered, after a little struggle with herself; for in her present mood his soul and hers would not be likely to come into very close contact.

"Anything but a boarding-house on a Sunday evening," he said, rather ungraciously, she thought. How many there were in that church who would have felt it a privilege to spend this quiet evening with her whose cheerful piety and wise words made her such a delightful companion to those who loved her. And he was only going to do it to get rid of the time! Well, she meant to keep her hold on Emily Wheeler's boy; one of these days he would thank her for it.

So they walked away together, he a little silent and pre-occupied; she bright and happy and talkative, and ready to fill his empty cup from her full one, if he would only let her. And after tea, when they were alone together, she won from him the whole story about Georgiana, and listened to all his tiresome expressions of disgust and vexation, a good deal as an angel would have done.

"You see, Aunt Jane, she has made me lose all faith in women; that's the hard part of it. For she certainly lured me on with such pretty little ways, such adoring little glances! Oh, you needn't ascribe all this to my vanity; her manner is indescribable, but it was such as no high-minded girl could possibly fall into with a man she meant to reject."

"I do not doubt it," was the reply. "And I can, perhaps, explain to you why you were so deluded by it. For the time, and in a certain way, she really liked you, and instead of concealing that liking, as under the circumstances she was bound to do, she made the very most of it."

"But *can* girls conceal such liking?" he asked.

"*Can* they?" repeated Aunt Jane. "Why, give them motives strong enough and they can hide and stifle their souls forever. And the most sacred instincts call them to do so; for it is not an unheard of thing for girls to give their hearts unasked, and yet in impenetrable secrecy."

"Do tell me something more about the dear creatures!" cried Horace. "It is delightful to think there may be a lovely maiden dying for me somewhere. I'm sure," he added, suddenly changing his careless tone for a serious one, "I wish there was."

"I do not see what good that would do you," said Aunt Jane. "But I sincerely wish and pray that you may find a true-hearted, loving, Christian woman to wife, Horace. You need it sadly. You are frittering away your life now, and need to have a new element infused into it. Or rather, two elements."

"And what are they?"

"I dare not tell you because you have protested against my preaching what you call sermons."

"Notwithstanding, say on," he returned.

"You need first, then, love to God. Don't interrupt me; I know you profess to love Him now. But you cannot pretend that this is the inspiration of your life."

"No," he said, laughing, to hide his embarrassment, "I certainly cannot and do not."

"And in the second place you want love to a pure, true woman, who will make a home for you with *her* love."

"That is true enough, at all events," he said, relieved that the dreaded "sermon" had been so brief. "But allowing that such a being, as you describe, exists on earth, where am I to find her. And if I find, what am I to do with her. Take her to my boarding-house?"

"By no means. Get a house and live in it with her."

"You might just as well say get a fortune, and share it with her. You know that I cannot afford it."

"I know that you have often said so, and to be sure, you cannot take a house in a fashionable neighborhood, furnish it richly, and establish a fashionable young lady in it. But if you would

once make up your mind that these mere outside
advantages do not touch the inner life in a single
point; that you want wife and children, and not
upholstery and style, I believe you could settle
down in a happy home forthwith."

The heart hidden away under the waistcoat gave
a great throb at the words wife and children;—
Horace was not spoiled by the life he had been
leading, though tainted by it.

"All you say about my needing a home is true,
Aunt Jane," he replied, "and you might say the
same of every young man in the city. But every
year makes our case more hopeless. Getting married is as formidable as getting to heaven; for my
part I have about given up all hope of attaining
either. Why, the ring a man offers his betrothed
when she promises to be his, must not be valuable
as the pledge of his affection, or as a sacred relic
of his past life, but intrinsically costly, so that his
Amanda can say to all her bosom friends, 'Behold
how many hundred dollars worth of Arthur's love
I wear upon my finger!'"

He spoke bitterly, and turned his mother's ring
about as it hung on his watch-chain.

"And then," he pursued, as Aunt Jane was silent,
"comes the wedding! and that involves another
visit to the jeweler's, and so on and so on; Amanda
must have her rich dresses and give her elegant

entertainments, and Arthur chooses she should; but if he happens to be poor, what then?"

"What then?" cried Aunt Jane, "why let him adapt himself to his poverty. Did Eve ask Adam to give her a palace to live in when he had nothing but a garden? And are there to be no weddings save diamond weddings—no homes save in ceiled houses?"

"It is all very well to talk," he said, glancing around the tastefully adorned room in which they sat. "But you, who have always been used to refinement and luxury, do not know how essential they are."

"I know that I, a poor girl, married a poor man," returned Aunt Jane. "And he took me to a home in which his love was my sole luxury, and mine my only refining influence. And how gladly I would go back with him this day, leaving behind me all that his long years of labor have won for me, into that *homely* home, if I might but go there with him in poverty instead of weeping for him amid this wealth. Oh! men make such mistakes! such fearful remediless mistakes! They sacrifice the lives on which other lives hang, under the delusion that when they are gone money can satisfy the aching, empty hearts they leave behind them."

This was the first time she had ever made the slightest allusion to a sorrow that had cast first a great shadow and then a great illumination upon her life. An illumination; for a shadow implies a sun.

"You must go now," she said, after a moment, "for I have got a little off the track, and don't know just when it was. But come again as soon as you like, and meanwhile, God bless you!" She gave him her hand with her usual bright smile, and he went away without a word.

CHAPTER V.

AUNT JANE was not surprised to see Horace march in the very next evening. She knew that she had touched, though she had not changed, his heart.

He began abruptly, with—

"Suppose a man could bring his mind to get married on his poverty, where is he to find a girl willing to share it with him?"

"A good wife is from the Lord," she returned.

"But do you know where mine is?" he persisted. "If I am ever to marry, of course there is somebody in the world waiting for me. Now where is she? Who is she?"

"If I knew I would not tell you. I hate matchmaking. You might as well ask me, where are my clients? Who are they? And I should reply, wait till they come to you and you will see and know."

"All I have to do, then, is to be ready for her when she comes! Really, I begin to feel quite curious."

"Yes, to be *ready*," said Aunt Jane, emphatically. "For if you are not, an angel might come to you and go away unrecognized."

"But ready, how?"

"In moral worth and purity, Horace." And after a pause, she added:

"If I were talking to some men, I should say: Ask God to make you fit for her when she comes, and then to send her."

"But why not to me?" he asked with a comical look.

"Because I know you wouldn't do it. You feel perfectly capable of choosing for yourself, and besides, you are not in the habit of taking counsel of Him in worldly matters."

"That's true, though how you found it out I can't venture to guess. You have the oddest faculty of seeing through a man. I shouldn't wonder if you knew just what I am thinking of at this moment!"

"Very well," she said, quietly, "you are thinking how you can get away gracefully from what you fear is an impending sermon."

The blood flew into his face; he started up quickly, and cried:

" I beg to go before you read any more of my thoughts. You are next door to a witch."

" I wish I could stay away," he thought, as he ran down the steps. "She'll get round me somehow, till she has me in some dismal little hole with one of her pious little girls, and then I shall have to black my own boots, and go to market and buy cheap pieces of meat, which will be cooked horribly by a slip-shod maid, and I shall lead about as prosaic a life as it is possible to conceive of."

But when he reached his room he could not help confessing that that looked prosaic, too. It had once been handsomely furnished, but everything had now a shabby-genteel aspect; and worst of all, there was nobody there to run to meet and welcome him. He felt unusually out of sorts, and wondered what ailed him, but on the whole laid the blame on Aunt Jane, whom he determined not to go to see again since she had such a knack at unsettling him. This turned out to be an easily kept resolution, for the next he heard of her was that she was very ill. He did not see her again that winter, and early in the spring she went away to her country-seat and spent a long summer there.

Meanwhile everybody, young and old, had been aroused and shaken by the civil war that sprang up as in a night, but should not cease till it had devoured in its cruel jaws, thousands of youthful lives, and left behind it thousands of broken hearts.

Horace Wheeler was one of the first to volunteer to go to the defence of his country. The true man in him, hitherto buried away under much rubbish, now came bravely forth into the light.

"Few could go so well as I," he said to Aunt Jane, when he went to take leave of her. "I have no mother or sister to weep for me if I fall, and I have my father's full consent and blessing. It is true I am his only son, but then I haven't been of much comfort to him, and we have lived apart so long that it could not make much difference to him either way. However, I expect to come back strong in life and limb."

"And suppose you do not? What then?" she asked, tearfully.

"Why then I make you my heir!" he returned, gayly, "and you will come into possession of all my law-books."

"Let us be serious in these last moments," she said. "I take a mother's place to you, in a certain sense, and if you never come back, if we never meet again in this world, where shall I look for you in the next, dear Horace?"

"In such a remote corner of heaven that you never will take the trouble to search me out," he replied. "Dear Aunt Jane, if I ever get there at all it will be through your own and my father's prayers, and not from any goodness of mine. You two have found more fault with me than anybody else in the world; it happens to be your very peculiar way of showing your love; but you pray for me far more than I deserve—and I'm not going away quite as thoughtless as you fancy."

This was the very most she could get out of him, and he rushed off as if ashamed and frightened that he had said so much.

So the great tide swept him away, and with him many and many a young husband, an idolized son, an only brother. And there were no wounds on the battle-field so ghastly as those that hewed down the hearts which bade them God-speed, and to this day there are no scars like those that many a woman is now patiently concealing. The havoc of life and limb caused by war is indeed fearful. But what of the havoc of human affections; what of the suspense, the sleeplessness, the unwritten anguish that turned many a sweet, peaceful home into a battle-field whose conquests and whose defeats were witnessed by no mortal eye?

The few friends Horace left at home, watched anxiously for news from him, and he wrote occasional letters, brief, sharp, and unsatisfactory. But he was distinguishing himself, and winning laurels, and when he came forth from battle after battle un-

harmed, he began to think that he bore a charmed
life. He had entered intelligently upon this sphere
of action; he was not fighting for his country and
enduring the privations of camp-life under a mere
impulse, but from a high and sacred purpose such
as inspired many another soul, and armed many
another right hand.

News-boys were crying papers all about the
streets, and Aunt Jane, sitting alone, and lost in
thought, at last heard the sounds. She rang for a
servant.

"What are they crying, to-night?" she asked, as
he entered.

"There has been an awful battle," he answered,
"I've got the paper, and Jim's one of 'em; mowed
right down, and killed in the twinkling of an eye;
see, here it is in the paper; there's no mistake
about it. And I hope you won't take it unkindly,
ma'am, but I'm going to fill his place."

"I am shocked and grieved at this news," she
said, "and Robert, you are not strong as Jim was.
Is it wise in you to go?"

"I don't know whether it is or not, but I promised him that if he was killed I'd just go and fill his
place. Them was his last words before he went:
'Fill up the places as fast as they're empty.' And
besides, I couldn't settle down quiet, now Jim's
gone. He was all I had." And the poor fellow

broke down, and retreated, leaving the paper behind him.

Almost the first words her eyes fell upon were these :

"Captain Wheeler of the New York 82d, missing." She had not heard of Horace's promotion, and at first hoped this might not be he. But a little reflection showed her that it was. She felt sick and faint for a moment, for what horrors might not this word "Missing" conceal? And then she began to pray for him mightily — no other word can do justice to the strength with which this woman laid hold on the Divine promises. She asked that if he lay wounded and over-looked upon the battle field, aid might speedily be sent him ; if taken captive that he might be rescued, and spared the wasting terrors of imprisonment. And then she waited patiently to see what God would do, and this is what she afterwards heard He did.

The battle had been a terrible one, and Horace, at the head of his company, had been in the heart of it all day; one of the most fearful and one of the most decisive days of the whole war. And while Aunt Jane was kneeling before God, pleading for his safety, as if he had been her own son, he lay wounded upon the field where he had fallen nearly twenty-four hours before. Who can tell the horrors of those hours? Or how many lives

3

he lived, how many deaths he died in them. At first his bodily sufferings benumbed his faculties; then they became absorbed in the eager hope of rescue; and when that hope gradually died out, and he knew that he must die there in all the flush of his strength and manhood, and die alone, a horror of great darkness fell upon him. He almost lost the sense of pain as the questions forced themselves upon him, "Am I ready to die? How do I know that I ever made my peace with God? What has there been in my life to prove it?" And a dismal answer came back to him, declaring that it was now too late to decide such momentous questions; too late! too late! And then he gave himself up to the fever and the pain and the exhaustion that claimed him as their own, and resigned himself to his fate.

"Come this way, doctor, here are half a dozen still living," said a voice near him.

"Oh, doctor, save me, save me!" cried a boyish voice, close at Horace's ear. The doctor stooped over the youthful figure and let the light of his lantern fall upon the face already becoming rigid in death. His lip trembled, as he replied, "My poor boy, it is too late. I can only take away those for whom there is yet hope. God bless and stand by you to the last!" he added, as he turned from him to Horace and examined his wound.

"I think this poor fellow may pull through," he said. "Take hold gently, Barnes, gently now; once safely in the ambulance we will do something for his immediate relief."

Horace felt himself lifted, and it caused him such an agony of pain that he wished they had passed him by.

"Leave me to die," he said, faintly. "I have no mother, no wife to lament me, and hundreds of these poor fellows have."

"We will save you, if we can, to gain in the future what you have not had in the past," was the cheerful answer. And then, amid untold anguish, Horace was jolted in a crowded ambulance, over a rough road, to the hospital; that is to say, to a church improvised for the time for that purpose. When his turn came, he was stretched upon the sacramental table (he remembered it afterwards with a sort of pleasure), and a surgeon clad in an apron hastily torn from the pulpit curtain, amputated the limb that had been mangled and crushed and neglected till it was past cure. He cared little what they did with him; as far as he had any thoughts about it at all, he fancied that the loss of a limb was a small affair, and wondered at himself that he was so indifferent about it.

But as the days of convalescence approached, indifference gave place to insupportable anguish;

he said to himself that death would have been a thousand times better. And then he yearned for his mother as he had never done since the first weeks after her death; he wanted to weep away his despair on a woman's breast, instead of hiding it in the pew where he lay alone.

"Have you no friends, Captain Wheeler?" asked the chaplain, one day; "no one to whom you could wish me to write?"

"Yes, I have two," he answered bitterly. "My father ought to hear, I suppose, and there is a friend of my mother's who would like a line, perhaps."

Four days later, when he had been removed to more comfortable quarters, there came to his bedside, a gray-haired, bright-eyed woman; and a wounded comrade, looking enviously on, said to the chaplain, who sat writing by his side:

"The Captain's mother has come to nurse him, and they have both been crying and hugging and kissing enough to kill a fellow who ha'n't got any."

"I had the impression that he had no mother," replied the chaplain, musingly; "but it seems I was mistaken."

"Oh, Aunt Jane!" said Horace, "what made you come!"

"I came because I came," she said, smiling

through her tears. "And now you must forget
that I am not your very mother; I might have had
my boy lying here wounded in your place if God
had not wanted him for some other purpose, and
taken him from me long years ago."

And then his father came, and for the first time
within his remembrance, Horace felt that here was
a heart that loved him.

Those were wonderful days in the hospital. He
did not now repel the wise, Christian words spoken
to him by the two who watched beside him; this
world was forever changed for him, and he was
thankful to have his thoughts turned from it. A
great deal of the time he was as docile as a little
child, drinking in the teachings his soul craved as
if he sat really at his mother's knee; at other times
the sense of what had befallen him would come in
upon him in such great waves of distress that his
two watchers could only weep with him.

"Death would have been so much better, so
much better!" he would cry at such times; and
then the tide, which can't be always coming in,
thanks be to God, would flow back, leaving a shore
behind it on which the form of His Son might be
almost visibly seen walking.

As soon as it was possible to move him, they
took him home; that is, they took him to Aunt
Jane's home, and the sorrowful-looking father

returned to his more distant one. As he took
leave, he uttered these parting words, with a tenderness that was the offspring of a remarkable
union to Him who spake them:

"It is better for thee to enter into life halt or
maimed, my son."

"Yes, it is better!" said Horace.

And so he had had his baptism of fire, and had
come out of it another man.

They had many pleasant talks together after this,
he and Aunt Jane, and she had reminded him of
the sympathy Jesus showed when on earth for the
"maimed," how often he healed them, what comforting words he spake to them, and how He
charged His disciples to remember them especially, when they made their feasts.

"Yes, I had thought of it," he said, "and it has
been a source of unspeakable consolation. The
time has been when I should have scorned to go
to a feast as an object of pity, but now I long for
human sympathy."

But with all the sympathy he received, and it
was not a little, he had to have his dark and sorrowful days; yes, there were times when "neither
sun nor stars in many days appeared," and no man
came unto him, for he would let no one come.

But at last he emerged from this great tribulation into the light.

"I am at peace now, Aunt Jane," he said. "I have done fighting with the Lord, and have put myself, just as I am, maimed and halt, into His hands. I could not have believed they were such tender hands."

There was one source of pain connected with his loss, of which he never spoke. But he had assumed, almost at the outset, that he never could marry. He fancied he should never have the face to ask a woman to limp through life with him; and yet there never was a time when he so longed for the home and the wife Aunt Jane had often pictured to him. His worldly ambition was gone now; if there was only somebody who was patriotic and unselfish enough to take him, just as he was, he would marry, and have his own fireside, and gather about it those who had rallied round him in his sore straits, and such waifs as were floating about as he had done.

In due time he was established once more in a boarding-house, an artificial limb partially supplied the loss of his own, and he re-opened his office under favorable circumstances. The Young Men's Christian Association opened its arms to him; he became interested in the once-despised Mission School, and once or twice his voice was heard at the weekly prayer-meeting which he never used to attend. He felt, at times, that he had gained

through loss; that he was a happier, better man;
and yet a voice often whispered in his ear; that
next to the love of God he needed the love of a
Christian woman.

CHAPTER VI.

HORACE had nearly recovered his youthful vigor, and was in the midst of unusual activity, when the illness of his father called him home. This illness proved to be sharp and brief, and ended in a peaceful death. Thus he was left without a single near relative on earth, and he took his seat in the train to return to the city, with a sense of isolation that saddened and depressed him. Life looked hard; it wasn't paying its way he thought; his lame leg was giving him a good deal of discomfort, or rather his artificial leg was. It seemed a dismal prospect to be always suffering thus.

He was in this mood when, at a wayside station, four young girls, escorted by a very assiduous young man, entered the train and seated themselves right behind him; or rather the girls did so. The assiduous young man arranged them to their liking and then withdrew. He had placed

3*   (57)

them face to face with each other, and as soon as the train moved off, they began to talk and to chatter and to laugh, as only American girls do talk and laugh in public vehicles, and he could not help hearing all they said, as did everybody around them.

"Can you ride backwards, Mag?" cried one. "And can you, Lou? How fortunate, for neither of us can endure it, can we, Nan?" To which "Nan" assented vehemently, and then there was a little whispering, till Nan, warming with her subject, began to talk quite loudly again.

"I'll tell you the whole story. You see, when he first proposed to enlist, she made a time about it, and said and did all she could to alter his resolution. But go he would, and go he did, and she gave him fair warning, that if he were maimed or disfigured or anything, she should break off with him."

"What a horrid thing she must have been!" cried Lou.

"Well—it wasn't as if she didn't give him fair warning. Do you think it was, Jo?"

"Jo" inclined to be non-committal. But on the whole, she should prefer, herself, to marry a man with two legs.

"Of course;" Mag here put in in a low voice, which Horace heard, however, for she sat just be-

hind his head, "but you see, they were engaged.
That alters the case. She had no right to break
off a solemn engagement."

"As to that, there was not much solemnity about
it, till our Mag must needs put her finger into
the pie. Well, to go on, by and by he comes home
with one empty coat sleeve, and a frightful great
red scar on one cheek. She fainted dead away
when she saw him, and it made her so nervous to
look at him, that he only went to see her occasionally. And then it got rumored about the village
that the engagement was broken off. Now comes
in the ridiculous part. Our Mag—"

"Don't, Annie, don't," pleaded Mag. "People
will hear you!"

"I'll speak lower, then. What does our Mag
do, but march to see her, and first coax, and then
upbraid, and then——"

"Oh, Annie! it isn't fair to tell that!" said
Mag's suppressed voice once more.

"Stop your ears, if you don't like to hear it, you
dear little goose, you! Our Mag got down on
her knees and prayed about it!"

"Well, well!" cried Jo and Lou in a breath;
while Horace felt like shaking them, for he was
sure that the unseen Mag was crying.

"I couldn't help it!" she said, "I pitied him so,
and he seemed so heart-broken. To think what

sacrifices he had made for his country, and how thankful a girl with a heart as big as——"

"A peppermint?" suggested Nan.

"Yes, as big as a peppermint," said Mag, waxing wroth; "how thankful a girl with the very least speck of heart would have been to spend her whole life in making him forget what he had lost."

"What sort of a man is he?" asked Lou. "Perhaps Maggie may console him herself."

All three laughed at this very witty suggestion, and Nan replied:

"Oh, no! he wouldn't do for Mag. He is a very common sort of fellow. We wouldn't let him look at her. But he'll find somebody, no doubt, before long. That's the way with men. Meanwhile we are going to carry Maggie off out of his reach, lest, what with her patriotism, and what with her pity, she should throw herself into his arms,"

"She couldn't do that; for according to you, he has but one arm," said Jo, laughing.

"I don't see how you can joke about such things," said Mag.

"They seem to me almost too sacred to speak of. Think of losing so much as one of your own fingers! For my part, I never see a wounded soldier without wishing I might say a kind word to him, if I could do nothing more."

"Oh, your fate is sealed," said Nan, "you'll marry the first one-legged animal that comes along, just out of pity. But if I were a man I should want to be loved for myself, not from compassion."

Miss Maggie vouchsafing no answer, the conversation thenceforth flagged a little, and at last the four girls relapsed into entire silence, and Horace was left to not a few mingled emotions. "Warm-hearted, and patriotic and gentle!" he said to himself, "and a girl who can get down on her knees; all this I know of 'our Mag,' and yet have not so much as seen her! She would marry even me, out of pity."

But at that thought he shrugged his shoulders.

"Passengers for Beverly will change cars!" shouted the conductor, a few hours later, whereupon great confusion arose among Horace's fair neighbors.

"Mercy on us! I had no idea we were to change cars!" cried Lou. "Where is my traveling-bag? Has any one seen my water-proof? Make haste, Jo, we shall be carried off as sure as fate."

So they were going off, and he should hear their gay talk no more; going away when he had not had a glimpse of one of them, especially "our Mag!"

"I dare say she's red-haired, and coarse and

freckled," he said to himself, " but I must and will
see her ;" and he started up with one of his most
graceful bows, and with an " Allow me to assist
you, young ladies," was right in the midst of them
in a moment.

"Thank you; and if you *could* reach down my
traveling bag, and if you would see if my parasol
has fallen under the seat; and, oh, thank you, that's
it !"

They were all mixed up together, so that he did
not know which was which, but he was conscious
of a sense of relief when he found that he was to
part company with only two; the lively "Nan"
and "our Mag" remained behind. The whole
scene occupied not more than three minutes, and
then the train moved on, and he gave a curious
look at the two sisters, who were absorbed in getting to rights after the flight of their companions.

At another time he would have been struck
with the brightness of the one face, and the sweet
earnestness of the other, but Maggie's surprised
glad smile of evident recognition quite startled him.

"Who is she? Where can I have met her?" he
vainly asked himself. But he had presence of
mind enough not to ask her, and he did not pretend to conceal that he was glad to see her, trust-
ing soon to learn, in conversation, who she really
was.

"I hope you have been well since I last had the pleasure of seeing you," he began hypocritically, and seating himself before her.

"Oh, yes, I am always well. This is my sister Annie; she has never seen you, but has often heard me speak of you, haven't you, Annie?"

"Very likely," returned Annie, coolly. "But I should know better if you would be kind enough to mention the name of your friend."

"Mr. Wheeler," Horace hastily put in.

"Then I can say, positively, that I never in my life heard you speak of him," cried Annie.

"Why yes, Annie; don't you remember? However, as I was never introduced to him, and, till this moment, never heard his name, except," she added, smiling, "his Christian name."—

"Horace," suggested our hero.

"Yes, Horace," said Maggie.

"Oh!" quoth Annie, looking very closely and curiously at him, "and so you are Horace?"

He felt not a little flattered that this sweet-looking Maggie had spoken of him to her sister; but how happened it that she remembered him, when he had so completely forgotten her? But as he did not expect to see her again, but to lose her as soon as the train reached the city, he determined to make the most of the time remaining. It was far pleasanter to chat with those pretty girls, and such girls! than to sit staring out of the window, getting his eyes full of cinders. And so he went on exactly as if they had been friends for years, and from a light skirmish they at last got into open warfare. Maggie had read everything there was to read about the state of the country, and had some very positive opinions of her own which did not agree with his. And though she was so gentle and lady-like in every look and tone, she would not yield to him an inch.

"But I ought to know, because I was in the army several years," he said, at last.

"In the army! Then why are you not in it now?"

"I was honorably discharged," he replied, and tried to change the subject, but she would not let him.

"I am so disappointed in you," she said. "I did not think you were one of the sort to get discharged while your country was still in such peril!"

Horace was embarrassed. After what he had overheard he could not allude to the occasion of his discharge, so he muttered something about being ill.

"Oh, but you are quite well now, are you not, and you will enter the army again, won't you?"

"That's the way she talks to everybody," said

Annie, naturally misunderstanding his increased embarrassment. "Mother often says she goes too far."

"One can hardly go too far in a good cause," he said, and there the conversation became less animated; he had evidently lost ground with Maggie, and she had less to say.

And now the train went thundering into the depot, and he had not learned who they were, and where they lived. It would have been better, he thought, if he had at the outset frankly owned his ignorance, but that wouldn't do now.

"We shall see you before long, I suppose," said Annie, as they parted.

"Certainly; that is—I should be nappy "—

"Oh! Annie did not mean that you should call on purpose to see *us*. She only thought you would be in and out more or less, while we are in town, and that will be several weeks," said Maggie. So their home was not in the city, as he had taken it for granted it was, and his chance of stumbling upon them by accident was limited to a few weeks. In his eagerness he ran after the carriage which was driving off with them, saying:

"But you have not told me where you are to be found?"

"At the same dear old place," replied Maggie, as the carriage drove on. He stood looking after it in no little perplexity. They would think it very strange if he should not call; and besides, they were nice, pleasant girls, and it was a shame to let the acquaintance end here.

CHAPTER VII.

WHY didn't I take a carriage and drive after them?" he wondered, and then he went home and pondered over the events of the day, and the strange conversation he had overheard, and asked himself what " our Mag" would say and do if she only knew on whose ears it had fallen.

"It would nearly kill the sensitive little thing," he said to himself, "and I'll not repeat a word of it, lest in some round-about way it should get back to her." These were among his last thoughts before he went to sleep that night, and this accounted, he fancied, for the fact that her image, sweet and fresh, came to him with his first waking ones next day. But why she should go wherever he went, why she should flit in and out of his office was not so obvious. He laughed at himself, said it would pass in a day or two, and entered into his usual pursuits with unusual ardor.

"I have got off the business track," he thought,

"by absence from it; and my brain is confused by the journey yesterday." But when he was riding up town after his day's work was over, she came into the stage, too, and when he sat down to dinner, she sat down by his side. Oh, Maggie, how could you? He tried to shake her off in vain, and as he knew Aunt Jane would be expecting him in the evening, he set forth for her house, and our Maggie went with him. Or rather, there she was at Aunt Jane's side, in a pretty blue dress; she and her sister Annie, in living form.

Conscious as he was of the way in which she had filled his thoughts all day, and quite taken by surprise by finding her here, he was thrown entirely off his guard, and stood before the two quite speechless.

But he soon recovered himself, and when he heard both girls address Mrs. Faulkner as "Aunt Jane," it flashed upon him where and when he had seen Maggie before.

"I hope, my dear *cousins*," he began, recovering his usual ease of manner, "that I find you quite well after yesterday's journey?"

"We are quite well, dear cousin," said Annie, laughing, "only Maggie is troubled with a few anxious fears lest you may have overheard some of our careless talk; but you didn't, I am sure?" Never was mortal man more tempted to tell a down-right lie. But he got off, for the time at least, by declaring—

"Of course I heard every word, and wrote it down in my journal before I slept."

"Ah, I knew you couldn't have heard," said Annie, "though to be sure, if you had, no harm would have been done." And then they passed a pleasant evening. Horace spoke of his father, and finding both girls interested, read a little record he had made of his pleasant sayings during his last days on earth.

"And you were just returning from this beautiful death-bed yesterday?" asked Maggie. "Then how our laughing and talking so near you must have jarred upon you!"

"On the contrary it quite diverted my mind from some sober thoughts," he returned.

"Then you did hear, after all!" she cried, crimsoning to her very fingers' end. "Oh, Annie, what did we say!"

"You spoke of me, for one thing," said Horace quietly.

"Now I know you did not hear," said Maggie, "for we never once mentioned you."

But she did not add, as she might have done, "I thought of you too much to speak of you," and after a delightful evening he went away in such an enraptured state of mind that he left his cane behind him, which made it necessary that he should go for it the next evening.

Meanwhile, he was becoming a marvel to himself. He caught himself twenty times while sitting in his office alone, or when passing through the streets, mentally conversing with Maggie; telling her his whole story, even confiding to her to what new and blessed heights of Christian faith and love he had climbed of late. And how he felt that he had her full sympathy, though he had heard only one little sentence about her that said she prayed when she was greatly moved, whatever she might do at other times.

"I never knew anything like it!" he said to himself at last in despair. "It must be that my father's death makes me tender towards everybody."

Yet it was not to commune with everybody that he presented himself at Aunt Jane's again so soon; it was only to get his cane.

Aunt Jane could hardly repress a smile when she saw Horace enter. For she had happened to see the cane in the hall, and knew it to be his, because it was her own gift to him, and she knew that dependent as he was upon it, he had not left it by accident.

"I hope the young ladies are well," he said, after waiting some time in the vain hope of seeing them make their appearance.

"They are quite well," she said, but was so cruel as not to explain the occasion of their absence.

"What a precious fool I have made of myself by coming this evening!" he thought. "For of course I can't come to-morrow; it would look too marked."

"I was going to invite you to dine with us to-morrow," said Aunt Jane, "and take the girls to church."

Horace started.

"Don't look so amazed," she said, "I only put two and two together. You left your cane last night as an excuse for coming again, and you have sat two minutes in perfect silence, meditating, instead of making yourself agreeable. One of my girls, or both of them, has caught you at last."

"Oh, no!" he cried! "Not but that they are pleasant girls enough, but"—

Aunt Jane smiled.

"Don't talk to me about 'pleasant girls,'" said she, "but tell me which it is you want? Why, hitherto you have been in such a hurry to come and boast of having fallen in love, that now I hardly know you." Then thinking she had gone too far, she added—

"They've gone to dine with Mrs. White. She has known them this long time, and is fond of them both."

Horace feigned indifference, and asked some trifling questions about a blue stocking that peeped
from a dainty little basket upon the table.

"That's Maggie's work," said Aunt Jane.
"What a pity that she forgot to take it with her!
We wanted to send off a barrel to-morrow."

"I should think you would need a hogshead instead of a barrel," said Horace, casting his eyes
about the room, which, like many a loyal parlor
during the war, was full of shirts, socks, handkerchiefs, in short, everything conceivable and incon-
ceivable that a soldier could want.

"So I told the girls when I saw the trunk they
brought with them.   They must have worked like
two beavers.   With all they have to do I can't imagine how they accomplish so much."

"Aunt Jane," cried Horace, abruptly, "do they
know about—about my leg?"

"I suppose so.   But let me think.   No, on the
whole I doubt if they do."

"They must have observed my lameness."

"Perhaps so."

"Unless they ask a direct question about it will
you be silent as to the cause?"

Aunt Jane looked at him with great surprise.

Was he going to try to gain the affections of
one of them under false colors?

But his honest face rebuked this unjust suspicion.

"It will be quite easy to be silent," she replied. "Both girls have too much delicacy to ask questions on such a subject.

"I should think one of them might have," he returned. "Do you know, Aunt Jane, that I have never been introduced to either of them, and do not know whether they are the Misses Snodgrass or the Misses Snooks?"

"Upon my word, then, you made yourself quite familiar last evening, calling them your cousins, and all that."

"But you know I had met them on the train, and overheard any quantity of lively talk on the way."

"Indeed? Then I am ashamed of you that you did not warn them that you were listening."

"Do you call it listening when a parcel of girls talk loud enough to edify the whole train?"

"Now I know Maggie Wyman never did that!"

"Perhaps Maggie in particular did not, but I know the young ladies in general did. How should I distinguish who said this, or who said that, when I sat the whole time with my back to them? And as to any little secrets I was so lucky as to hear, I should scorn to repeat them."

"Secrets indeed! Maggie Wyman shouting her secrets into the ears of the whole train!"

"Indeed, Aunt Jane, I never insinuated that she

4

did. So, I am to come to dinner to-morrow night? I wonder if I can? I half promised to dine with Ben Lowell."

"Very well, dine with him then and welcome," she said, demurely.

"Oh, I dare say he'll let me off. Yes, I'll come. Anything to please you. Where did you pick up these fair maidens?"

"Oh it's a long story, and I can't go into details. I have known them ever since they were little girls. After the death of my husband and my son, my health was all broken up, and I wanted to get out of the city into some quiet place, where I could brood over my grief. This, you know, was before I purchased my present country seat. I advertised, and friends made inquiries for me, and at last I somehow wandered off to a little mountain village whose chief attraction lay in the fact of its obscurity and isolation. The father of these girls was the minister of the single church there, and he began to come to see me. I had never met such a single-hearted unworldly man; at the very first interview he did me good, though somewhat younger than I. Then he brought his wife, and by degrees they roused me from the despair into which I had fallen, and gave me my first conception of a 'heart at leisure from itself.' I was boarding at a common country tavern, amid many dis-

comforts, and really suffered for want of many
things that my ill-health made necessary. Almost
every day, therefore, one or both these girls, then
six and eight years old, came to bring me something prepared for me by their mother's own
hands. She did it from the purest kindness and
sympathy; inferring that poverty only could in-
duce me to take up my abode in such poor quarters. I naturally wanted to make some return,
and as my health began to improve, proposed that
the little girls should come to me for daily lessons.
This proved to be as great a benediction to me as
to them; I learned to love them dearly, and they
filled up and kept warm some of the empty places
in my heart. The whole thing ended in my going
to the parsonage to spend summer after summer,
and gaining in the beautiful Christian home there
a new conception of this life and of the life to come.
Mrs. Wyman was not one of the sort who could
say much on religious subjects with her lips, but
she said many things in her life; and Mr. Wyman
preached Christ to me as truly out of the pulpit as
in it. I never can repay the debt of gratitude I
owe them both. We feel a very peculiar gratitude
towards those who are a spiritual help to us; don't
you think so?"

"Indeed, we do!" he said, warmly. "Think
what you were to me down there in the hospital."

"The girls," she went on, "proved to be charming little scholars; I never tried to do anything with the boys; they were younger, and, besides, I couldn't manage them; they were always startling me with their noise, and I really had no health with which to bear what their mother only laughed at. As Maggie and Annie grew older, I sent them away to school for several winters, one at a time, for their mother could not spare both at once. This winter Mrs. Wyman has a sister with her, and so she could let them come together, and I want them to have a right good time; they deserve it, for they have a hard life of it at home."

Horace hoped she would go on all night, but at this point in her discourse it became necessary for her to set the heel of a great blue stocking she was knitting, and she warned him that he was not to speak while she counted her stitches and performed that mysterious act.

"Why, how is this?" she said, suddenly, "my yarn is giving out! I thought I wound enough to last a week. I shall have to steal some from the girls. Hand me that large ball, and I will wind, or rather you shall wind off, a part of it for me. Have you a bit of paper about you? Or stay, here is an envelope in the work-basket, you can wind upon that. Meanwhile, excuse me a moment, I must look for the mate of this stocking."

Horace took the envelope and was proceeding to fold it in such a form as would make it available for his purpose, when his eye caught the word " Horace" written upon it in pencil; he colored, and looked about him with a guilty air; it had come from Maggie's basket, would she miss it, must he return it? Another glance revealed the address in a free, manly hand—" Miss Annie Wyman." It wasn't Maggie's after all, then? At any rate there could be no harm in keeping it; that one word "Horace" told no secret, and yet it somehow seemed to entitle him to keep possession of the mutilated paper on which it had been hastily scribbled. He lost no time, therefore, in thrusting it into his pocket, substituting another for it, and when Aunt Jane returned she found him so clumsily at work in winding her ball that she snatched it from him.

He was now quite eager to get home to study his prize at his leisure, and set his face in that direction, with a light heart. Yes, there it was, in a graceful, very original hand, his own name, over and over and over again; but whose hand had traced the word? Annie's, no doubt, he said, with a sigh; but then didn't the paper come from Maggie's basket, and hadn't Maggie meant to take that basket with her? The envelope had evidently had yarn wound upon it, for it folded, almost of itself,

into a compact, square form; it did not follow that
she who had written his name upon it cared for
him a fig; but yet this looked like it. Perhaps it
was Maggie after all; perhaps she had begun to
forgive him for leaving the army, and was beginning to—well, to what? He dared not ask; and
then the image of a poor, disappointed fellow,
with the empty coat-sleeve and the red scar, came
and whispered, "Why shouldn't my name be
Horace, as well as yours?"

It is amazing what mountains we make out of
mole-hills when we are in love; into what Kohi-
noors we can transfer grains of sand.

CHAPTER VIII.

WHEN Horace presented himself at Aunt
Jane's the next evening, at five o'clock,
he was told that the dinner hour had
been deferred till six, as the barrels des-
tined for the army were not yet packed, and the
dining-room was in confusion.

"Aunt Jane says you may come and help us, if
you like," said Annie, after delivering this message. He followed her, therefore, to the dining-
room, and though it hurt him not a little, made
himself very useful. The girls were in high spirits,
and made themselves merry over their work: still
Horace felt that Annie treated him with evident
friendliness, while Maggie kept out of his way as
much as possible. Indeed, he did not know what
to make of Maggie: every now and then in the
midst of her gayety there would come over her a
fit of gravity and silence that suggested some
secret source of unrest. At last, when the barrels

were full and some articles still remained on their hands, Annie said:

"Now, Mr. Wheeler, jump into the barrels and crowd the things down; we must have room for these magazines and papers; some of the poor fellows in the hospital will be so glad of them."

Horace cast a look of despair at Aunt Jane; his jumping days were over; but must he tell these girls so, and get them to liking him out of mere pity?

Aunt Jane understood the look, and came to his rescue.

"He is not half heavy enough," she said; "I will call John; John will answer the purpose far better. Meanwhile, Horace, suppose you write the address of these barrels on cards. Maggie, dear, can you find some cards?"

"Yes, here are some," she said, "and here is the address, just as I took it down when General Walton gave it to us."

Horace almost snatched the paper from her in his eagerness to see this specimen of her handwriting; his spirits sank when he found it quite unlike that in which his own name had been written so profusely. He had been, up to this moment, so full of life and joy, that every one observed the change in him. The truth is that this trifling incident suddenly revealed to him how enchanted he

had been at the bare hope that Maggie thought of
him long enough at a time to write his name even
once, and if she had done it from mere idleness.
As to Annie—of course it was she—why all she had
done it for was to show what wonderfully graceful
H's she could make!

"Mr. Wheeler is very moody, is he not, Maggie?" Annie asked the next morning, at breakfast.

"Is he?" said Maggie.

"Yes; and did you notice how he limped, last
night? I have no doubt he wears tight boots."

"Very likely," said Maggie. She seemed a little
pre-occupied, and unlike herself. The sudden
change of manner that had come over Horace
when she gave him the address, at Aunt Jane's
request, had been too striking not to make an impression upon her. "What had she done to annoy
him?" she asked herself, and then reproached herself for caring, and then said she did not and could
not care for a man who, in this hour of his country's peril, could keep out of the army if he tried.
Yet she watched for him, evening after evening;
whenever the bell rang, she fancied he had come;
but he came not. Then she grew gentler and
sweeter than ever, and Aunt Jane wondered that
a man who had seen her, as Horace had, could
help loving her; and said to herself that she had
cast this pearl before swine. She had proclaimed

4*

herself as hating match-makers, and she was trying to be one as hard as she could.

"To think of his not so much as calling, after
the dinner I got up for him!" she thought, with
secret indignation. "Does he really imagine that
such girls as these grow on every bush, and can
be had for the asking?" And so she let Mrs.
White's great darling, good-natured Tom come
where Horace should have come, and tried to
fancy that he would "do" for Annie, at least. And
Annie laughed at and bewildered and captivated
him, and Maggie listened to his prosy talk with as
much deference as if it had been all alive with
gems. Thus, when Horace at last made his appearance, he found them. Annie, who made no
secret of her liking for her "cousin," as she usually
called him, immediately left Maggie to entertain
the wearisome Tom, and began to call him to account for his neglect.

"Only to think," said she, "you are our own
cousin, and have not been here for ten days!
What have you got to say for yourself?"

"A great deal," he returned, "if I choose to say
it. But I don't intend to do so. Now, let me ask,
why you hav'n't been to see me?"

Annie laughed, and said she had thought of it,
but didn't know where he lived; whereupon, with
mock gravity, he gave her his card.

"I do believe," thought Maggie, "that he is giving her his photograph! It would be just like Annie to ask him for it." And she looked at her sister reprovingly, making signs that she must behave herself. Annie subsided a little, but as soon as Tom White regained Maggie's attention, she began again, talking as if she had known him all her life, and with a friendliness, an evident liking for him, that might well have turned his head.

Aunt Jane was greatly scandalized. She had never seen Annie in such gay spirits, nor looking so attractive; it would be just like Horace to be caught by this bright girl, and just like Maggie to know so little of her own worth as to put up with Tom White. And Horace, with the firm conviction that he had made an impression upon her, and that Maggie was more than indifferent to him, wavered a little; that is to say, he acknowledged that Annie was easier to get acquainted with than Maggie, and very amusing and entertaining.

Meanwhile Tom White sat on pins and needles; he hardly heard a word of what Maggie was saying, but was trying to hear what was going on on the other side of the room. He did so envy Horace the animation with which he was able to respond to Annie's; did so wish he were as handsome, as easy and graceful!

When the young men took leave, Aunt Jane

told them they might come the next evening, if
they chose, as she was going to have what she
called a " Busy Bee." This proved to be a host of
young girls equipped with needles and thread,
who were to make up material provided by her for
the soldiers. Horace hardly spoke to Maggie; he
did not know what he expected her to say and do,
but, at any rate, he was dissatisfied with her; she,
on her part, scarcely looked at him, but while busy
with her work, let Tom White, who could not get
near Annie, sit by her side and weary her with his
dullness. At last it so happened that the scenes
changed; Tom and Horace were called upon to
scrape lint, and Annie and Maggie were sent for
old linen for the purpose. When they returned
with it, Horace had an opportunity to vent his
growing discontent on Maggie. If he had known
in what an unreasonable mood he was, he would
not have spoken at all; as it was, he said, with a
smile, intended to cover the irritation with which
he made the remark:

"You have acquired such ascendancy over Mr.
White, that I wonder you have not sent him into
the army."

Maggie made no reply, save by a quick glance
of surprise and pain, which he misinterpreted.

"She likes him!" he thought; "I have seen it
all the evening. I thought she had more sense."

"Excuse me, I entreat," he added aloud, "if I had really dreamed that matters had gone so far."—

"What matters, and how far?" asked Maggie, with some spirit, and yet not unkindly.

"I really haven't a word to say," cried Horace. "But I hope you will not let such an unintentional piece of carelessness give you pain."

"It was not unintentional," she replied, looking up to him, "you know it was not. Yet I am ashamed of myself for caring. But sometimes, in some moods, we are over sensitive, and a grain of sand will then tear and rend as a mass of jagged rock could not do at another time, or in a different mood."

And then she disappeared; whether through the floor or through a door, Horace, in his confusion at what he had done, did not know. He was ashamed and angry with himself; the whole thing had sprung up in a moment, and now he stood perfectly bewildered where she had left him. He felt that he had settled it forever, that she should dislike him; yet, never had he realized, as now, how much she had become to him. Indeed, she had raised herself in his eyes by showing that her extreme gentleness was not a mere negative charm; that she could be roused and inspirited, and made to resent a wrong without any unchristian anger.

When Maggie disappeared from his view she meant to speed to her room as fast as her feet could carry her, and have a good cry. But a horror of being cross-questioned about it by Annie, who would be sure to find it out, and just as likely as not to tell everybody that our Mag had been crying,—this made her control herself, and go steadily to work, as far off from Horace as she could get. She seated herself near a group of girls who were making themselves merry over a gray shirt, which some body had apparently cut for Goliath of Gath.

"We might all get into it," said one.

"It will do for a shirt and a blanket in one," said another.

"Captain Wheeler says that the great fault of the garments sent to the army is their enormous size," said a third. "Poor fellow! they say his artificial leg hurts, at times, dreadfully, and I have no doubt it does to-night, for I just saw him leaning against the wall, looking pale and haggard."

"He has never been as strong since he lost his limb as he was before," was the reply.

Maggie's heart stopped beating. How many times she had told him that she was ashamed of every young man, in good health, who was not in the army—and all the time he knew that he had given his country all he could! She was not usually impulsive; she was in the habit of taking counsel with herself before she took a decisive step. But now she rose with a quick, energetic movement, that said she must not lose a moment, crossed the room, and stood before Horace with a kindling face.

"I have misjudged you cruelly," she said, with difficulty keeping back the tears that filled her eyes. "I never knew you had been wounded; if I had I should have honored and " *loved* you for it, she came near adding in her excitement.

"Don't speak to me, don't look at me!" he said. "I thought I was ashamed enough before, but you have annihilated me now."

She could not trust herself to say any more, and returned to her seat, where she found Annie had joined the group, and was listening to a detailed account of the battle in which Horace had lost his limb, and all about his heroism at the time.

"It made another man of him," said Clara Reed, biting off a thread. "He used to be so worldly and so fond of fashionable society; and now he is as good as he can be."

"I mean to go and ask him to tell me all about it." said Annie.

"Don't, Annie;" cried Maggie, holding her back; "you'll say something to annoy him."

"Something that will annoy you, you mean,"

said Annie laughing, and breaking from her. " I'll promise not to breathe your name."

So she pumped him well, and he told his story in a manly way, that would have been brief had she allowed it.

" Well," she said, gayly, at last, " I suppose you don't mind it much. You've got the glory and the honor; and it's so nice that you don't have to go on crutches; why, I never dreamed that anything ailed you, except that you wore tight boots, and Maggie said—oh, but I promised Maggie that I wouldn't lisp her name, so I can't tell what she said, but it was something nice. Oh, it wasn't about you; you needn't think it! Don't you like our Maggie? But I forget; you do not know her; and considering how intimate you and I are, it is a little queer that you don't know her as well."

So he and Annie were intimate, were they? Putting this statement by the side of the scribbled envelope, Horace felt his blood run cold. Next news he should hear was that he was engaged to her. And he had never liked her so little as at this moment, when she could rattle on about the tragedy of his life as she would talk to a wooden doll that had lost the tip of its nose.

Yet, Annie was by no means the heartless girl he was at the moment disposed to believe her to be. She was inexperienced, and thoughtless, and impulsive, and had seen very little of the world; that was all.

Aunt Jane espied Horace standing alone and apart from every body not long after, and saw that something was amiss. She went up to him kindly, and asked him if the evening had wearied him.

"No; he said, "the *evening* has not."

She saw that he did not want to be questioned, so she left him, and very soon the young ladies began to prepare to take leave, and there was a deal of laughing and talking as they at last went off in twos and threes.

Horace knew he ought to go too, yet lingered. If he could only get one more look from Maggie, and could only force her to forget how rude he had been. But he got neither word nor look. She was hard at work gathering up the various articles over which the girls had been busy, folding, sorting, and carrying them off in her arms, as if this had been her sole business all her life. But Annie hovered round him, full of gay talk; she had forgotten all about the loss of his limb, and only thought how handsome he was, and how nice it was to have him like her so.

Horace went home in the comfortless state of mind familiar to those who have been left to do, in one or two little sentences, what they feel they cannot undo in a lifetime. There are few warm-hearted people who do not sometimes say in their haste what nothing would tempt them to say at their leisure, and then how they chafe under the sense of their own folly.

"How could I rally her about Tom White!" said Horace to his forlorn self. "She must have seen how horribly jealous I was. It's all up with me; she says I did it on purpose, so, of course, she thinks I deliberately went to work to annoy her. I'll keep out of her way henceforth; as for Annie, why couldn't *she* have taken to Tom? I'm sure she could make something of him if she'd only take him in hand."

He held good to his resolution to keep out of Maggie's way till the following Sunday, when he went to church with his heart all in a flutter at the idea of sitting in the same pew with her. But he found only Aunt Jane and Annie there, and pretended he was glad of that, since his mind would not be withdrawn by her presence from the real object that had brought him to the house of God. And then that gladness was dispelled by Maggie's coming in a little late, and with a lovely color suffusing her cheeks as he rose to let her enter the pew. She had some books in her hand, that showed she had been to some mission school, with Tom White, no doubt, but he enjoyed having her sit next him for all that. Indeed, he was so conscious

of that enjoyment, that when the service was over
he dared not look at her; he felt that every body
would know how he loved her if he gave her even
so much as a glance, and so he walked away. Yes,
how he loved her, for he could no longer conceal
from himself that she had been hardly out of his
thoughts since the day he had heard her sweet
and earnest words in the train, four weeks ago.

CHAPTER IX.

THE next day he received cards for Miss
Fitzsimmons' wedding, which was to take
place in a fashionable church, and a note
from that young lady, requesting him to
act as groomsman on the occasion. He was seriously annoyed, yet to refuse was impossible, and,
as an interview was necessary, he had to call.

"All the handsome young men have been killed
off in this horrid war," she said, as they met, "and
Hattie Foot is such a beauty that I wanted her to
have you to stand up with."

This *quasi* compliment did not melt the hard
heart with which Horace stood before her; so he
had got to be set over against Harriet Foot, and
would be thought to be returning to her set.

"Aunt Jane will be sure to bring them both to
the wedding," he thought, "and what will they
think?" And then he suggested to the bride elect
that it would not be a very graceful progress up
the broad aisle of the church, if he came limping
in the procession.

"Oh, that need not trouble you!" she cried, "I like to display my hero friends! We chose you on purpose, Hattie and I. It is all the fashion now to make much of those who have fought for our beloved country."

So there he was.

"I wish I could get married to-morrow;" he thought, "if only to escape this farce. Our beloved country, indeed!"

And then there had to be a rehearsal of the marriage ceremony before that ceremony took place, and he got all mixed up with the old set in such a way, that he felt like a fly caught in a web.

At last the wedding day arrived, and Miss Fitzsimmons, all lace and diamonds, was made to promise to love and honor an insignificant looking little man, with his hair parted in the middle, who looked not a little frightened, as well he might. No one would have suspected who witnessed the scene in the church that day, that a fierce and cruel war was raging in the country; the display of dress, and fashionable array of spectators, offered a fearful contrast to the poverty and wretchedness, covering as with a gloomy pall so large a part of it. Horace reproached himself for participating in this pageant, and his heart wandered away from the elaborate lady on his arm, to a little modest figure, that he felt must be there, though he would not have profaned her by a look if he had known where.

Quite late in the evening, after the brilliant bridal reception was over, he encountered Tom White in the supper-room, who blushed like a girl as he asked if he could have an interview with him next morning. Fancying he had gained a new client, Horace named an early hour of the following day, and went home jaded and out of spirits. The world he had just left had never looked so hollow and unsatisfactory; he hoped he should never have to enter it again.

At the appointed hour Tom White made his appearance, and after any amount of circumlocution, finally blurred out his business in this wise.

"I say, Captain Wheeler, we can't both have her, and I can't endure this suspense any longer. I made her acquaintance before you did, and never cared for any body else. Now, I'll act fairly and squarely if you will. You may propose first, and if she accepts you, I'll retreat, and leave the field to you. If she refuses, I want you to quit it, and let me try my chance, which is poor enough, I know."

Horace thus challenged, knew not what to say Must he own his secret to this Tom White? But then that young gentleman had already taken possession of it.

"I think," said Tom, waxing bold, as he saw that his rival shrank from him, "that if I can be frank and speak out, you can. It will not cost you any more than it does me."

"But it is not the thing," said Horace, "to make proposals to young ladies in their absence from home. You must at least wait till they return."

"Oh, that is an old fashioned notion," cried Tom. "My mother, who is the pink of propriety, says that their aunt has given her sanction to my plan; that is as far as it concerns myself; of course I have not compromised you."

"Let me suggest then that you take the matter into your own hands. Propose to both of them, if you choose; I will not stand in your light. You can offer a position that it is not probable I ever can do; and at all events I am not prepared or disposed to pay my addresses to any young lady at present."

"I ask your pardon, then," said Tom. "I had quite the contrary impression. And really, when I come to think of it, and realize that whatever your feelings are towards her, she has such a preference for you, I hardly dare to take a step in the matter. But before you made your appearance she did seem fond of me."

"Indeed!" said Horace, dryly, and with great inward disgust.

"Yes; don't you think it is a little particular when a young lady gives you her photograph?"

"Why, yes, decidedly so," said Horace, burning with secret rage.

"To be sure it was done in a hasty moment, and she wouldn't accept mine in return, but laughed at me for offering it. Indeed, she is always laughing at me, as you must have seen."

"May I inquire of whom you are speaking?" asked Horace, to whom it suddenly occurred that it did not seem like Maggie to be always laughing at anybody.

"Why, of Miss Annie Wyman, of course," replied Tom.

"Ah, well, my dear fellow, that field is quite open to you. I have no thought of addressing that piquant young lady, and if she was fond of you once she is no doubt fond of you still. Go ahead. I wish you all sorts of good luck."

He was so relieved that he could hardly help hugging Tom; and Tom could have leaped for joy.

"I'll do it," he declared, "the first chance I get. Or at least as soon as I get courage." And then the new client walked away, and Horace drew a long breath.

"If he does not care for her why should she care for him?" he thought. "I'll go to-night and watch her more closely than ever."

And so he did. But Maggie met him with apparent indifference. She had seen him figuring in a worldly scene, apparently quite at home in it, and felt more out of sympathy with him than she had ever done. She had been led to believe that since the loss of his limb he had cut himself off from fashionable society, and devoted himself to all she loved best. But here he was, at a gay wedding, with a stylish, elegantly dressed young lady on his arm laughing and talking with her as with one with whom he felt on equal terms. She believed the pain this gave her was due to the sense that his Christian tone was lower than she had fancied it; in a measure this was true. But perhaps some lower sentiments mingled unconsciously with the higher ones; perhaps she felt that he who could choose the society of a Harriet Foot, could hardly really value her own. Yet the contrast between her serene face and modest attire, with the scene he had witnessed and shared in at the wedding, was making her dearer to him, and he knew it. That scene had revealed to him how changed he was since the days when he used to seek happiness among them; how much less and yet how much more he expected from life.

Annie, meanwhile, was as attentive to him as ever, full of gay and fearless talk like one sure of the ground on which she walked, but as silent to-

wards Tom White as Maggie was towards him
For Tom was there, as large as life, swelling with
his secret, yet close at Maggie's side, for if she
wasn't the rose hadn't she dwelt near the rose?

"Our Mag is going home to-morrow," Annie
said, at last. "One of the children has the measles
and of course they'll all have it. And she thinks
mother will need one of us to help her through
the siege."

"Why don't you go, then?" asked Horace, vexed
to think of losing sight of Maggie.

"I can't tear myself away from you!" she returned, laughing.

These words ought to have fallen upon Tom's
ears like balm, for they could not have been spoken
in that open way by one whose heart secretly belonged to him she addressed. But he was obtuse
enough to take them literally, and to become so
down-cast that everybody was relieved to see him
soon take himself off. The four then drew close
together around the fire, and talked of Maggie's
departure; Horace now learned for the first time
that she lived in the little town of Stafford, four
miles off the railroad.

"Do you make the journey alone?" asked
Horace.

"Oh, yes; Aunt Jane sends John with me to the
station, and he gets my ticket and sees me off, and

my father meets me at Grafton; we have then only the four miles drive."

The next morning beheld the unaccustomed sight of Horace Wheeler arraying himself for the day by gaslight, and seven o'clock found him at the station just as Maggie, a little behind time, came driving up. She gave a great start of joy when she saw him; but he did not see it, and as it did not suit him to be recognized by John, he skulked off.

"How could I be so foolish?" Maggie asked herself. "Why should I fancy, even for a moment, that he came to see *me* off. But then he may have come for Annie's sake." John, having seen her safely in her seat, at once took his departure, and Horace instantly appeared. He had had no special design in coming, had made no programme, did not know what he meant to say. There were only a few minutes before the train was off, but in those few minutes both were so embarrassed, said such stupid things, that in after days neither could recall a single word. But he went away a happy man, for the time, at least, and the train hardly dashed more rapidly on its way than did Maggie's joyous heart.

"Maggie has come home nicer than ever," said the hero of the measles to his brother that night.

"She couldn't be any nicer!" was the reply.

"She kissed me twice when she went away, but she kissed me four times when she got back," persisted the hero.

Ah, you foolish little man! It was not you she kissed!

"It was not necessary for you to come home, Maggie dear," said her mother.

"I thought it was ; besides, I wanted to come." And so she slipped into her old place, the same, yet not the same, hardly daring to whisper to herself the sweet secret that had been but half betrayed ; wondering if she had betrayed her own, the knowledge of which had come to her in a sudden flash in those few trembling minutes on the train.

It was one of those stormy nights on which Horace chose to visit Aunt Jane, with the hope to have her all to himself. For this little old lady with her bright ways and straightforward yet not unkind words, was in great demand, and it was long since he had had a private interview with her. But now he knew that Annie had gone to dine with Mr. White's mother, and that her dangerous ears, so ready to prick up at the sound of news, were safely out of the way. And he had made up his mind to open his heart to Aunt Jane like a son.

But it was not easy. He did not know when or how to begin, and set holding the ball from which she was knitting, in his hands, wishing she would speak first.

"Aunt Jane," he at last got out, "you are so skilled at reading my heart, that I don't believe it is necessary to tell you what is in it."

"No," she replied, with much feeling, "you need not. There are many good things in it, and among those good things I see my little Maggie; do I not?"

"And do you think there is any chance for me?"

"Ah, that is a question I cannot answer. You know I have often told you that girls have a great knack at keeping their likings and dislikings, to themselves."

"What am I to do, then?"

"Why you are to act in your usual straightforward way, and write and tell her how you feel, like a man."

"Oh, I couldn't write. I must see her. I am going to Stafford to-morrow, unless you advise against it."

"But I do advise against it. You'd catch the measles."

"I've had them."

"Maggie will not be able to see you. Those boys are her regular tyrants when they're sick."

"There's another thing I want to consult you about. A friend of mine has a paper in his posses-

sion on which his name is scribbled some score
of times. Should he presume that the lady who
wrote it, did this because she particularly cared
for him ?"

" If he is as modest as most men he will presume
it, whatever I may say. I should advise your friend
to put that paper into the fire, and think and speak
of it no more. Such a document might be the result of mere idleness."

Well, an old, crumpled, yellow envelope is not
much of a "document," save in the hands of a
lover, and Horace mentally followed Aunt Jane's
suggestion.

" But, notwithstanding the measles, I am tempted
to go to Stafford," he went on, and upset a vase of
flowers on the table to show his zeal.

" At all events you need not sop up water with
one of my best handkerchiefs ; or what is better
you need not upset my vases."

" I ask your pardon, Aunt Jane," he said so
meekly, that her kind old heart yearned over him.
" I did not observe that it was your handkerchief."

" I have heard that love is blind," she replied.
" Well, if you will go, let me post you up as to the
trains. You will go by the early one, six or half-
past six ; you will reach Grafton in time for the
stage to Stafford. You'll take your supper at the
tavern, get yourself up in your most enchanting

style, and reach the parsonage a little after seven.
You will find no one at home save Mrs. Wyman
and the boys.   Mr. Wyman will be at the prayer-
meeting down in the cellar of his meeting-house,
and Maggie, after nursing the boys all day, will be
there, too ; I know her mother's ways well enough
for that.   So you can chat with mamma till they
get home.   By the by, I hardly think you know
what a truly religious girl my Maggie is."

"A single sentence on that head was my first
attraction to her," he replied, lingering with his
hat in his hand.   "I could not love a young lady
now, who was not truly and deeply religious.   Oh,
Aunt Jane, how you have changed me !"

"How *God* has changed you, you mean.   To
think that a simple little country girl like Maggie
Wyman has won the heart that none of the attractive young ladies here, with all their advantages,
have ever touched !   Good-bye, my dear boy, I
congratulate you, and myself, too, in advance."

"Thank you for those kind words," he said, with
much feeling.

He had not made up his mind to the step he was
now about to take, without much reflection and
much prayer.   It was a very serious, weighty thing
with him ; so different from his proposal to Miss
Fitzsimmons, that he shuddered to think what
would have become of him if she had accepted him.

But he was resolved to be very cool and quiet with Maggie, so that she need not be moved by compassion to accept him. And if she refused him he meant to be yet more cool and quiet, and never let her know the pain she had given him. On his journey he tried to think how he should manage things, provided he should find Mrs. Wyman at home and alone, as according to Aunt Jane he was likely to do; should he introduce himself and tell her his errand? What, speak to a perfect stranger of the secret he had guarded so jealously, that he had found it so hard to reveal to his second mother, Aunt Jane? His beating heart warned him to lay no plans, but to trust itself to Providence, and let it have its own way.

Meanwhile Maggie was enacting the sweet daughter and sister, unconscious that he about whom she quarreled so much with herself was every moment drawing nearer. She had a habit of holding silent conversations with him, which vexed her extremely; as she moved about her household tasks and sat at the long seams she had to sew, or went up the village street on her little errands, she was telling him all she ever did, and then detecting herself in it, would break off suddenly with great confusion and self-reproach. To-day she fancied she had gained great dominion over herself in this respect, for she had no such

temptations; but the truth was, the children had
made her read to them, or tell them stories so dili-
gently that she had not had time to think.

"Maggie, dear," said her mother, "I want you
to go to meeting to-night, it will do you good after
being shut up all day."

"But they say you can carry the measles about
in your hair," returned Maggie. "I can change
my clothes, but I can't leave my hair at home very
conveniently."

"I think that's all nonsense," said Mrs. Wyman.
"Besides, there won't be any children there this
cold night, and all the grown folks are safe."

"And I can sit near the door and slip out without speaking to any one," said Maggie, who really
wanted to go.

She usually went to the evening meetings in her
every-day dress, which was simple enough, but as
she had now to change it, she put on a pretty blue
one, in which Horace had seen her, and she well
remembered his saying that girls should never
wear any other color.

"Here he is again!" she said to herself. "I am
so ashamed of myself I don't know what to do!
How he would despise me if he could see my
thoughts!"

She slipped into the lecture-room and took her
seat in a dark corner, feeling very little in her own

5*

eyes, and intending, as she had said, to slip out
and come home the instant the meeting was over.

But she came out into the darkness with her arm
in a man's arm, her hand clasped in his hand, trembling, flushed, triumphant. How they managed it
no mortal knows. What he said to her, if he said
anything, he never told; she never could tell what
she said to him, for she did not speak a word. The
very utmost that could afterward be got out of
either of them was this : that Horace happened to
come to meeting, and happened, which was true,
to step into the seat near the door, where she happened to be sitting, and what was more natural
than for him to see her safely home?

Maggie frightened her mother not a little by
tumbling into her arms and bursting out crying,
but it did not take long to tell the rest of the story,
and to make up a fire in the parlor where Horace
sat freezing, and introduce him as Aunt Jane's particular friend.

And then they took him right in with such delicious simplicity, never cumbering their heads with
the question how their country ways would strike
him, and loving him right off because he loved our
Maggie! He went through the form of spending
his nights at the tavern, but there was precious
little formality of any other sort. Maggie took
him into the kitchen and made him break eggs,

which, however, she would not trust him to beat; introduced him to the nursery and constrained him to tell stories about his army-life; and invited him to shovel a path for her to the well. If he loved her when she sat quietly and demurely in Aunt Jane's parlor, how did he feel now that he saw what a gladsome, happy little creature she was; perfectly at ease, kindly affectioned towards everybody, yet reserving the depth and the tenderness of her nature for him alone!

Aunt Jane, Annie and Tom White, were sitting together one evening, at the close of the week, Annie behaving like one possessed, Tom cast down and silent, when in came Horace. All rose to meet him, when, without ceremony, he took Aunt Jane in his arms and kissed her and then Annie.

"I left them all well at your house this morning," he said to the astonished young girl. "Ah, Mr. White, I'm very happy to see you," and looked as if he would kiss him too.

"You have been to Stafford? Been at our house?" cried Annie. "Don't go, Mr. White," she said, seeing that young man about to make a precipitate retreat. "And what did they say? "Do they want me to come home? Did you see Maggie?"

"I did see Maggie!" he returned in a tone that told his story; whereupon Annie began to cry.

Tom White's heart concluded to begin to beat again, and Aunt Jane cried and laughed and called herself an old fool.

"Sit down and tell us all about it," she said at last.

"I have lived a year since I saw you," he replied, "and it would take a year to tell about it." But he began his story with great animation, and the eager talker and the eager listener did not observe that Tom and Annie had miraculously disappeared.

"I thought he was in love with you," said Tom, "and that is the reason I never dared to speak out. And I thought you loved him. Indeed I don't know what I didn't think. And when he rushed in just now and caught you and kissed you, I came near fainting away on the spot."

"I never would have forgiven you if you had!" she declared. "And how absurd it was in you to fancy I cared for him, when you might have seen, only you are such a dear blind old goose."

Well, it is not fair to listen any longer. It suffices that two more souls had got into that earthly paradise wherein lovers have walked ever since Adam and Eve walked in the garden, perfectly convinced that there never was any experience to be compared to theirs.

And now, having conducted Aunt Jane's hero

and his heroine to the threshold of a new life, shall we discreetly leave them to cross it alone? Or shall we cross it with them and look into the prose that follows the poem or is there to be another poem and no prose?

CHAPTER X.

THE year that had opened so eventfully for Horace and Maggie, proved to be the final year of the war; and the first beautiful days of October were celebrated in the little Stafford parsonage by two simple weddings; both Maggie and Annie were to leave the home where they had spent their happy childhood, and sail forth upon an unknown sea. Indeed, Annie was to do this literally; for Tom was going to take her to Europe, and she was in a state of great bewilderment between him and his presents and his radiant delight over her.

Maggie, on the contrary, was going to be established in an obscure street, the wife of a poor man; she was going to meet with embarrassments and endure privations; lonely hours lay before her, and hours that would require all her courage and fortitude. But she was more than fearless; she was thoroughly happy. To live with Horace! What could she ask beside?

When his marriage was decided on, Horace had many consultations with Aunt Jane, inclining to the opinion, which she was always ready to fight, that with his limited and uncertain means it would be best to give up the long-talked of little home.

"If we live in that street nobody will come near us," he objected, when Aunt Jane, after endless drives, had at last found a house in which he could afford to live. "Besides, I want to put Maggie into a spot more worthy of her."

"Yes, but you can't live like a rich man and at the same time be a poor man."

"I know. But this is such a low, vulgar sort of street. And the house looks worthy of the street."

"Yes." There was a pause of some moments.

"The truth is, I want you to set an example to the hosts of young men who are living unsatisfactory, bachelor, boarding-house lives. In nine cases out of ten pride lies at the bottom of these lives. Because they can't begin where their fathers and mothers left off, they won't begin at all. They dry up and stagnate for want of an object. Look at Ned Long. He is a man of real talent; if he had a wife and children, and were forced to exert himself, he would make his mark in the world. As it is, he contents himself with just making a living. Am I not right?"

"Yes, you are. But if I had a wife and half a

dozen children, I should not work harder than I do now. So your remarks do not apply to me."

"Because you are expecting a wife. Now I know that I am urging you to a career that will require very great moral courage. And I know that it was easier for you to face the cannon's mouth on the field of battle than it is now to face what people will say. We are cowards, all of us, sad cowards."

This roused him. "I'll take the house," he said, with decision. "After all, it is nobody's business how and where I live."

"And Maggie is so unworldly, and loves you so, and is, besides, so independent, that she will be just as happy in an obscure as in an aristocratic street. And now as to the furnishing of this house, what sum can you afford to spend upon that? For of course, Maggie's father can give her very little besides his blessing."

"I have what my father left me at his death. Where he lived, and as he lived, it was quite a sum. In this city it is next to nothing at all." And ashamed to speak the words, he wrote the figures on a card and handed it to her.

"Why, this will do nicely!" cried she. "You must remember that Maggie has been used to very simple things, and that she will content herself with very few."

"I am sure the parlor at the parsonage was as pretty as a picture," said Horace.

"Yet there is not an expensive article in it. Its pleasant home-like air was given it by the girls. They have both some taste; Maggie has a good deal, and you, too, can have a parlor 'as pretty as a picture,' if you will let me send for her and let us furnish your house to suit ourselves."

"I shall be only too thankful," he said.

So Maggie came the happiest little thing to be imagined, and showed that she had as wise a head as she had loving a heart. She would not so much as look at such upholstery as Horace had fancied indispensable to house-keeping, but cut and planned and fitted with her own hands till she had made a little bower of bliss out of the house whose outside looked so shabby, and that was so home-like within. Horace was not allowed to set foot in it, but was obliged to live on what faith he had in Aunt Jane and in Maggie, till he brought the latter home as his wife, and found himself sitting with her at their own cosy breakfast table.

"Why, what have you done to this old house?" he cried. "It looks as fresh and cheery as this bright morning! I am sure Aunt Jane has slyly used her own purse, in addition to ours."

"No, that she hasn't!" cried Maggie, in great triumph. She sat opposite him looking like a rose

—a pink, not a red rose—and he took her in as a part of the picture that satisfied and gladdened his eyes. He was so happy, this little home was so different from any home he had ever known, that he fancied he had never been happy before. He could reach across the small table and catch her hands, and did catch them; if they had been red once they were not red now, though somewhat plump and childlike.

"And now must I leave this little paradise and go off to my office?" he said, as they at last rose from this their first meal together as husband and wife.

"Not yet," said Maggie, "we haven't had prayers yet, you know." And she brought the Bible, her father's parting gift, and placed it in his hands.

He had not thought of this; it startled him a little, as suggesting that he was now at the head of a household. Yet the thought was pleasant; he felt himself twice the man he had done, as he took the book from his wife, and the simple, almost boyish prayer he offered, as she knelt by his side, came from a very happy, thankful heart.

It is not necessary to tell how many times they took leave of each other that morning; perhaps nobody knows. But at last he got away, and Maggie watched him till he was out of sight, and would gladly have gone with him if she might.

And now, if she had been at a boarding-house, she would have had a long, tedious day before her. As it was, she had dinner to order, and her trunks to unpack, and many a little touch to give the rooms they had occupied.   And the dinner was a study. She wanted everything to be agreeable to Horace, yet knew she had precious little money to work with.   Fortunately, she had never in her life known what it was to get along save on the strictest economy.   She thought of many things she knew how to make to perfection, but was astonished to find she must not make them, because milk and eggs, the great staples at home, cost so much here.   And when she went into the kitchen to consult with the angelic being there, she found her to be far more human than divine, and not at all disposed to an invasion of her domains.

" I thought," Maggie began, " that I would have a beefsteak pudding for dinner, for one thing, and—"

" There ain't no beefsteak left," quoth Biddy.

" Where is it, then?"

" Gave it away."

" Don't do that again, Biddy.   We shall have to live economically, and everything is very high."

" I don't think I shall suit," quoth Biddy.   " I ain't fond of economical ladies, nor of stingy ones either.   I can't live to a place where they begrudge a morsel to the poor."

"We don't begrudge it," said Maggie, unruffled; she was too happy to make herself wretched about trifles. "But we choose to give what we have to give with our own hands, not through yours."

"I don't think I shall suit," repeated Biddy, and chipped the edge off one of the new plates by banging it into the dish-pan.

"Very well," said Maggie. "You need not stay unless you choose. I know how to do everything that is done in a house, and I can get my husband's dinner as well as you can; and shall enjoy doing it, too."

"She ain't easy to put down," reflected Biddy. "I thought she was so sweet-spoken that she hadn't no spunk. But there's only two of 'em; its an easy place, and I'm agoing to stay." And then she produced the beef-steak, which she had only given away prospectively to one of her numerous "cousins," and paid some heed to Maggie's directions about dinner, though with a lowering countenance, and a further injury to plates and platters.

Here was prose with a vengeance.

"I'll get along with her, somehow," thought Maggie. "It is foolish to let such little things annoy one." But she was annoyed, and when she went up stairs and found in what a slatternly way her room had been summarily arranged, she was annoyed again, for there were the marks of two dirty hands on the new white quilt, and of the same soiled fingers on both doors.

"After this I will take care of my room myself," she said to Biddy.

"Suit yourself," was the glum reply. "I ain't fond of chamber-work." But the next morning, as she was sweeping her room, after the final litter of unpacking, Biddy marched in with a white tarleton dress over her arm, and a host of pink ribbons in her hands.

"Look here, change work, will ye? I've got the dress to trim against a ball to-night, and can't make the bows to suit me." Maggie was perfectly bewildered by the audacity of this proposal.

"Oh, Biddy!" she cried, "do you spend **your** hard earnings for such finery as this?"

"I suppose its nobody's business how I spend 'em," returned Biddy.

"I don't approve of young girls like you going to balls," said Maggie. "Think how much more respectable it is to stay at home and sew and read, and dress according to your station."

"I can't read, and I ain't fond of sewing."

"Let me teach you to read, then!" cried Maggie, eagerly.

"It ain't no use. And them ladies as thinks **a** poor girl as has worked hard all day, ain't to have no fun when it comes night, ain't no ladies."

Maggie made no reply. What would Horace think, if, when he came home at night, he found her getting dinner instead of flying to meet him, nicely dressed, as he expected? She felt herself under bondage, and Biddy felt it, too.

Aunt Jane came an uninvited, but very welcome guest, to lunch, and as she had secured Biddy's services, she made all sorts of inquiries that brought the whole truth to light.

"Dear me, this won't do," said she. "Mrs. Crane gave her an excellent character. But you want a quiet, respectful servant, not one of these wild, saucy young things. Never mind, let her stay her month out, and then dismiss her. I suppose, dear, you expected to meet with trials?"

"Yes, Aunt Jane, but not just these. However, one can stand anything for a month."

"And how is my boy?"

"Horace? Oh, he's well, and as happy as possible. You ought to have seen him when he came home last night! however, I'm glad you didn't. And he's so good to me! I'm getting so conceited and silly!"

"It does me good to hear it," quoth Aunt Jane. "But don't expect too much. Horace will have his hard days and you'll have yours, it won't always be sailing on a glass sea; but you must determine to be happy whatever betides."

But they sailed on something very like it, week after week. Biddy aggravated Maggie, and a good many people aggravated Horace, but when he came home at night to the cosy little parlor and the loving little wife, and they had their simple dinner together, and he sat on the sofa with the plump, yet elastic figure cuddled close to his side, he felt that he could defy the whole world, and she forgot that it had any Biddies in it.

There was peculiar tenderness in Maggie's love for her husband; he could not conceal from her that he suffered, and this made her demand less from him than young wives are apt to demand; made her give him far more than he ever dreamed of asking.

So evening after evening slipped by. Sometimes they lived over again those few weeks when a mysterious power was attracting them to each other, never wearying of those little details to which no third person could listen in patience, and sometimes lost in that delicious silence which is communion still. They did not want to go anywhere, nor to have any one come to see them; yet there were two evenings of each week which broke in upon these luxurious habits; one was the prayer-meeting, and on one they dined, regularly, at Aunt Jane's.

So the month slipped away, and Biddy was replaced by a modest-looking maiden, who moved about as if she had a cannon-ball tied to each foot, but who soon began to love her quiet home, and to serve Maggie with real devotion.

"I hope you will be contented and happy with us," said Maggie, when Mary made her appearance. "If anything goes wrong, come right away and tell me. Are you fond of reading?"

"I don't think anything will go wrong," said Mary, looking admiringly at the sweet face that smiled on her so kindly. "I'm always contented where families is kind to me. Yes, I'm very fond of reading of an evening, when my work is done up."

"I hope you won't be wanting to go to balls and such things," said Maggie.

"Oh, no, ma'am. I'm a quiet body; too quiet, folks says," she added, with a smile.

"Horace," said Maggie, lifting her head from his shoulder, that evening. "I want to say something to you, if I can only get courage."

"Well, say on, little one," he returned.

"I've been thinking that we've been living in a horribly selfish way since we were married."

"That's what we got married for," he replied, laughing.

"Oh, no; or, at least, that wasn't all of it. You know how much we used to talk about being hospitable, and opening our doors to people who lived in boarding-houses, or people in trouble. And you haven't been to mission-school since I came here."

"I know it," he said. "But it has been so nice and cosy here at home. Oh, Maggie! you can't imagine what it is to live year after year in other people's houses, eat at their tables, go in and out with nobody caring when you do it, and where you go!"

"No, I can't imagine it," she said. "But, Horace—"

"Well, dearie!"

"We haven't been living at all as I expected to live. I had a picture of our home in my mind before I came here, very different from the reality."

"Go on," he said, tenderly.

"Do you mind my speaking out?" she asked. "Will you promise not to be hurt or offended?"

He satisfied her with sweet words, or something that took the place of words, and she went on, glad that the room had not been lighted, and that he could not see her face.

"I thought we both were so much in earnest, so really and truly consecrated to God, that our loving each other would in no wise defraud Him. But I was mistaken. We give all the time we can snatch from other duties, to each other."

"But He gave us to each other, did He not?"

6

"Yes, yes! but not to decrease our love to Him."

"You are getting morbid, Maggie, dear. Surely we love Him no less, after all His goodness to us, than we did before?"

"I don't like to pass judgment on you," she said; "but I *know* that I love him less. I have been completely absorbed in you; you have been the atmosphere I breathed, and my heart has risen to fever heat, or sunk to zero, at your pleasure."

"Well?" he said, complacently, and drew her nearer, but she gently freed herself.

"And before I loved you I could have said that of my Saviour, and now I can't."

Horace was startled by her earnestness.

"You are a little darling," he said; "twice as good as I am. Don't go to accusing yourself. I do not see how such a tremendous event as a marriage can take place without a convulsion. You will get back again to where you were before."

"I hope so," she said; "but it will not be by accident, nor without your help."

"The helping will all come from the other side," he said. "I shall lean on you, Maggie, my pet."

Maggie was disappointed. She had fancied that if she once broke the ice, she should get a hearty response from Horace, and that they should at once begin to walk, hand in hand, in a new life together. After a time she said:

"It says in the Bible that 'the husband is the head of the wife, even as Christ is the head of the church;' and that 'Christ gave Himself for it that He might sanctify and cleanse it.' And this is what I thought you would be to me; what you would do for me."

Horace gave a long, deep sigh.

"No wonder you are disappointed then. Maggie, you little women who stay at home, and have nothing to do but to be as good as angels, can form no idea to what temptations we men are exposed. We are driven into the world; we see its worst side; we breathe its air, and become assimilated to it. And instead of coming home to set ourselves up as examples, we want to find our examples waiting there for us."

"We may not have *your* temptations," replied Maggie, "but we have our own; temptations just as peculiar to us and just as hard to resist, as yours are to you. For instance, take any warm-hearted girl, who marries for love, and in nine cases out of ten, she will make an idol out of her husband. Now this idol may have a more agreeable, plausible aspect than the ugly idol called money; but the one shuts out Christ just as effectually as the other does."

"Now you are talking just like a book."

"I didn't mean to," said Maggie humbly.

" You dear little thing !" cried Horace, " you are determined to turn me into an idolater."

And then they sat quietly side by side, hand in hand ; Maggie was frightened at herself, and happy in her husband's love ; after all, what more did she want ? So this evening slipped away as others had done, and the day ended, like all their married days, by their offering their evening prayer, together, and offering none apart.

On the following Sunday the morning sermon was on family life, and the preacher laid great stress on several points on which neither Horace nor Maggie had reflected before, especially on its individuality. And he drew a beautiful picture of a home which had Christ for its central object, while all else was subordinate to Him, contrasting it with one where self reigned under a refined mask, yet reigned still.

" There is nothing individual or characteristic about our little home," said Maggie, on their way from church. " I suppose there are thousands just like it."

" I doubt if there are a thousand Maggies," returned Horace, " and to me the word home means Maggie."

She smiled gratefully ; she always thought it condescending in people to love her, and then she said :

" Dr. Philips must have a delightful home of his
own, or he could not have drawn such a picture of
one."

" That does not follow. It is said that shoe-
makers' children always go unshod. Indeed, I do
not believe that such a home as he depicted exists
anywhere on earth."

Maggie made no reply. The sermon had im-
pressed her greatly, and she determined to act
upon one part of it immediately ; the hints in regard to servants. She had already invited Mary
to come into prayers, and Mary had made no reply,
but had not accepted the invitation. So she made
one more attempt, while attending to some little
point connected with dinner. Mary colored, but
answered respectfully, yet very decidedly, that her
religion forbid her doing so.

" But we pray to the same God, the same Saviour, that you do," urged Maggie.

" The priest forbids it," said Mary. " And I
never go against his orders."

" Very well ; then we 'll try, you and I, to see
which will serve God most faithfully in our different ways. And you must not be frightened if I
speak of Him now and then ; I shall not try to
shake your faith, but to strengthen it ; if you love
Him, and if I love Him, it will seem natural to say
so, sometimes ; won't it ?"

"I declare I could have stood and heard her talk all day," Mary afterwards confided to a friend. "It's a pity she is a Protestant, but there is some good ones among 'em." And while she was wiping away a few tears, Maggie was reproaching herself that she had not spoken more wisely, and eloquently, and tingling with fear and shame. This little effort to acknowledge Christ in her household reacted, however, upon her own soul; she had not felt so strong in Him since her marriage. Something she fancied lost had come back to her, and as she was running about after dinner, putting the room in which they had dined to rights, and turning it into a parlor again, she burst out into such a joyous hymn that Horace was quite surprised.

"What's come over the little woman now?" he cried, from the sofa, where he had been lying, half asleep.

"Oh, Horace, if you only knew! If I only could tell you! But I can't, only that I'm so happy!"

And then she slipped softly away to her own room, and begged the Lord Jesus never to let her get away from Him again, and he heard, and answered her. So that night when Horace said he was unusually tired, and wanted to get into his nest early, she found courage to say what she had been wanting to say all along.

"Horace, dear, I'm afraid we've both forgotten, in the new delight of praying together, what the Bible says about praying in secret."

"But we are one now, dearie," said Horace.

"Yes, in a sense we are. But in another we are two, and ought to have things to say to God, we can't say to each other. And I want you to let me go upstairs half an hour before you do: then you can have the parlor to yourself; Mary goes to bed at nine, and no one will interrupt you."

Horace replied by taking her in his arms, without a word. She stood leaning against him some moments, never dearer to him than now that she had owned to a higher allegiance, and he never knew what it had cost her to do it. But from this moment she was more cheerful and more loving than before, and so more lovable, and he needed a part of his quiet half hour at night in which to thank God that he was no longer homeless or wifeless.

CHAPTER XI.

'M awful sorry, but I've broke a plate," proclaimed Mary one morning, when Horace was giving into Maggie's hands the usual scanty supply for household expenses.

"I am sorry," said Maggie. "For Biddy broke two, and chipped the edges of several more."

"I just let 'em slip out of my hands: the suds made 'em slippery, and down they went," pursued Mary; and it turned out the one broken plate meant three, so chipped and scolloped as to be unfit for use.

"And I'm sure I don't know how it happened, but here's all the cuffs and collars mildewed; it's just the weather; and my own is among 'em."

"Mary do try to be careful," said Maggie. "Mr. Wheeler only gives me just enough for the table, and nothing for wear and tear, how should he when everything in the house is new?"

"He's a nice gentleman," said Mary, "and won't mind giving you a little more. Though I'm awful sorry I've been so unlucky."

Maggie looked troubled, Horace was finding it
hard to keep up even their simple little establishment ; he had owned that, when she had laughingly told him he kept her too short of money ; and
now there were plates to buy and new collars and
cuffs to be got. And such perplexities were constantly occurring.

Mary was faithful and economical, and devotedly
attached to her young mistress, but she would
make sour bread every now and then, and had a
regular habit of breaking the china and scorching
the table linen. Every body knows what fearful
prices had to be paid for the real necessaries of life
at this time, and how hard many who had been
almost rich found it to live. Without saying much
to each other about it, both Horace and Maggie
was getting careworn. He was afraid he would
not make enough to meet inevitable expenses, and
she was afraid she was extravagant or hadn't a faculty of getting along with a little. Yet she was
really doing wonders, if she had only known it.

On the evening of this particular day Horace
came home a good deal out of sorts. He had had
a most unpleasant business encounter for one thing,
and a couple of hundred dollars lent to a friend,
and now due, was not forthcoming. He must have
it when quarter-day came round, and it was coming as fast as it could, and his friend declared, with

6*

tears, that he would pay it by that time, but the case seemed anything but hopeful. He did not mean to trouble Maggie about it, and told her so when she at last got it out of him.

"Dear me, what is a wife good for if she mayn't cheer a man when he is downcast?" cried she. "You have said more than once that you did not decide to get married till you had asked God to direct you about it, and don't you suppose He did? You are not sorry you are married, are you, dear Horace?"

"*Sorry!*" he repeated, and snatched her from the low seat she had taken at his knee. "Why, it wasn't living before I had you!"

"But having me you have increased your cares. Hadn't we better break up house-keeping and let me go home till these high-prices come down?" she asked, demurely, and well knowing what he would say, or rather, what he would do.

"It is for you I care," he said, after a time. "I hate to keep you ground down so and to give you no luxuries."

"I call it a luxury to have a husband," she said, laughing. "I'm sure that isn't one of the necessaries of life—or wasn't a little while ago. Dear Horace, I did not expect anything I have not gained. I am more than happy, more than contented, and I do not believe we are going to want for any good thing. My father always said he hoped his children would begin at the little end of life."

"You've cheered me up wonderfully," he declared. "I came home feeling such a weight on my mind!"

"If worst comes to worst, I can let Mary go and get a little girl to run on errands, and have a woman to wash, and do the rest myself. So don't worry till I come to the end of my resources. Why, if you can't afford to keep this house, we'll move out of town where we can have a cheaper rent. We are not tied to New York."

"I don't know about that," he said. "I'm lamer than usual to-day and need to be nearer my office, instead of going farther from it."

And then Maggie was all tenderness and was down on her knees in a minute before the suffering limb; oh how literally on her knees, for much as she loved her husband for himself, here was a tie between them only less sacred than death.

"I want to have Aunt Jane to dinner to-morrow," said Maggie, when Horace felt easier in body and mind. "You know we haven't had her all this time, except to lunch, and then she didn't see you."

"Yes, I know. But could she put up with our plain ways, after her own luxurious table?"

"She never has a 'luxurious table,' except for visitors. And nothing could be plainer than the style at our little Stafford parsonage, and she spent several summers there."

"I should so like, though, to spread an ample table and exercise a large-hearted hospitality," said Horace.

"So should I," returned Maggie, "but I'm not going to make myself wretched because I can't. I know Aunt Jane will love to come, and I am ashamed that I have let a silly pride prevent my asking her. Or rather, pride and selfishness, for it has been so pleasant to have you all to myself that I have not wanted anyone.else."

So Aunt Jane came, in one of her best and sweetest moods, and they had a simple little dinner, ever so much pleasant chat, and some loving, motherly words from her at parting, that did them both good.

It cost Horace something to take down the family Bible and say, "we have made up our minds, Maggie and I, to have prayers directly after dinner, Aunt Jane, and she says visitors must make no difference."

But when he had said it there stole over him such sweet peace as he had never known in all his life before: both Aunt Jane and Maggie caught its tone in the prayer he offered, and wondered whence it came.

At the close of the evening, as the young husband and wife stood alone together before the parlor fire, Horace made confession to Maggie on this wise:

"Do you know, dear, I wanted to put off having prayers till after Aunt Jane had gone? Was I ashamed of Jesus, or what was it?"

Maggie looked up in great surprise.

"Why, when you were in the army were you ashamed to show your colors?" she asked.

"No, I was proud of them; proud to flaunt them in the very face of the enemy."

"And Aunt Jane is not an enemy," said Maggie.

"I have always had this shyness," said Horace.

"It is strange," said Maggie, thoughtfully. "For in ordinary worldly matters you are not shy."

"But don't you think it is natural to conceal our deepest, most sacred thoughts and feelings?"

"Thoughts and feelings are one thing," said Maggie, "and acts are another. It seems to me it would sound very oddly for a soldier to say that his patriotism lay so deeply in his heart, that he must hide his colors. Dear Horace let us show ours."

"But Maggie, darling, in those days when I secretly loved you, I could not have spoken of it to a living soul. I hid my love with the most jealous care."

"Yes, while it had so little vitality that you *could* hide it. But how much of a secret did you make of it when you stood at my side and proclaimed that you would love, honor and cherish me till death should us part, in such a decided 'I will!' that everybody in the church heard it."

Horace smiled. "Yes, and I would do it again!" he cried, "if I could get a chance."

"And if our love to Christ has in it real life and force, won't it speak out just so? Can it hold its peace?"

"I never knew till now what a coward I had been," said Horace. "I positively thought that I shrank from betraying my love to Christ—for I do love Him, Maggie! because it was so sacred a principle. I think now that its poverty and its infancy kept it silent."

"I think I understand you," said Maggie, after a little silence. "You have been mixed up with people who shuffled religion out of the way, as something to come in play on one's death-bed, but as unfit to mix up gracefully with daily life. How little I thought when I saw you at Miss Fitzsimmons' wedding, that you would ever be anything to me! How I fought against myself that day for admiring you!"

And then, of course, Horace said some of the foolish, yet passing sweet things he was wont to say to his little wife, and she found it hard to get away from him to that retreat up stairs that was the tower of all her strength.   Left alone, Horace thanked God for giving him this wise, fearless, loving wife, never so dear to him as now when she had tacitly rebuked his cowardice and revealed him to himself.   And as to Maggie herself, in a few sweet child-like words, she asked that she and her husband might walk hand in hand heavenward, *keeping step*, and told her Saviour about the perplexities in which he was involved, exactly as she would have told the story to a dear earthly friend.   She went to sleep serenely, and without a care ; wondering why she had suffered herself to grow anxious and troubled, when she could cast herself on One who had control of all the silver and the gold on earth.

But the next day brought new difficulties, and as if in mockery of the pressure on their domestic life, came a long letter from Annie, who was wandering over Europe without a care, indulging herself in all sorts of luxuries, and having, as she declared, the nicest time in the world.

"Think now, if you could have some of these nice times !" cried Horace.

"With Tom White ?" asked Maggie, in a tone that said all the most insatiable heart could ask.

And yet, after a little, Horace fell into a reverie,

now only too frequent. The incessant petty economies he was forced to practice, wearied him ; by
nature he was disposed to ample expenditure both
for himself and others, and hated everything small
and prosaic.

"Do put away that work!" he said at last, a
little impatiently, "and come and talk to me, Maggie. Surely you can do your needlework during
the day."

"Yes, I can," she said cheerfully, laying aside
her work. "I was only doing a little for our sewing circle. We call ourselves poor, and make a
great time about it, but just fancy living upon four
hundred dollars a year, as the Western Missionary
does for whom we are now working."

"You might as well say fancy our living in
an Irish shanty, or in one room in a tenement-
house."

"Well," said Maggie, "I could be happy in an
Irish shanty, or in one room in a tenement-house,
provided I could keep it clean. Dear Horace, you
can put on as long a face as you please, but I am
going to be contented and in good spirits as long
as I stay in a world where I can experience what
I have done to-day."

"And what was that?" cried Horace, rousing
himself.

"If you won't think it just my silliness, I'll tell

you. After you went down town this morning, and I had started for the day, (ah, what taking counsel of God was involved in Maggie's doing that!)—I tried to think what I could do in the way of comforting somebody besides myself, and what I should do it with. You are so fond of soup made of old bones, that I hadn't a scrap of meat to spare, and "—

" Now, Maggie, that is adding insult to injury," said Horace. " It is bad enough to give a man nothing but soup for his dinner, without insinuating that he is charmed with that arrangement."

" It doesn't hurt one to fast occasionally," retorted Maggie, who was proud, with reason, of her soups. " Besides, you had a nice bit of beef-steak after it."

" A bit, indeed !" he cried.

" I am glad I am not such a carnivorous animal as you are," she returned. " Why, you ought to see all the fresh meat eaten in my father's house in the course of the year."

" But it would be far better for him if he left off his pies, his doughnuts, his tea and his coffee, and had a good generous slice of beef or mutton in their place. You are behind the age, my dear, or you would know where his headaches come from."

" Am I ? Well, go back to the point. I had

heard, through Mary, that there was a family nearly opposite, where a sick child was dragging out a weary little life, sometimes lying alone all day while her mother was off at work, or gossiping with the neighbors, and I thought I'd just run over and see it."

"Well?" asked Horace, as she paused.

"I don't believe I can tell it," she said, trying not to cry. "Oh, Horace! We call ourselves poor and we chafe under our little cares and economies, and if we dared, we should say we wondered why the Lord kept from us the luxuries he gives so many others?"

"You'll get hardened to the horrors of city life," said Horace, laying his hand tenderly on her head.

"That I never shall!" she cried. "To think that that poor little child, only a stone's throw from our dear little home, was lying there all alone, with nothing on, literally nothing but a small shawl; no fire, no bedstead, no food, no compassionate loving words, nothing for companionship, but its sufferings, its dreariness, its hopelessness! And I had gone there empty handed!"

"And what did you do, my darling?" asked Horace, greatly touched by Maggie's emotion.

"There was only one thing I could do. I hadn't brought her anything, and I hadn't a word to say,

and I just took the poor little creature in my arms
and kissed her, till my tears wet her thin, white
cheeks. And the two arms flung themselves round
my neck, and the child clung to me as a drowning
man clings to a straw, and with such a wail of grief
and joy and loneliness and gladness."

"And then?"

"And then I knelt down with the little figure
still in my arms, and thanked the Lord that if he
hadn't given me money, or eloquent lips, He had
given me a heart warm enough and big enough to
take in and love and cherish hundreds of such children, yes, and hundreds upon hundreds."

"Come, my Maggie, stop crying," said Horace,
"and I'll live on soup all the days of my life."

"All the soup in the world wouldn't have put
the life into that child's breast that love and sympathy did," she answered. "Only to think!" it
kept saying, "a lady has kissed me!"

"I don't wonder at her delight," said Horace.
"I can remember a time when if you had come
and caught me in your arms and kissed me"—

"Hush, you foolish boy! Well, you won't look
disgusted if I pinch you a little at your breakfast
to-morrow, will you? For I came home and stole
a part of it, and made a little broth for the starved
creature, and Horace, we're not poor! We're rich,
just as long as we've got two loving hearts beat-

ing in our bosoms, and can defy any living creature
to ask more from them than they can give."

"Yes, we are rich," said Horace. "Or, at least
I am, in the dearest and best little wife that ever
crossed a human threshold."

Your FREE Catalog is ready and waiting for you!*

Just complete and mail us back this card.
Or for faster service—
Call us, toll-free, at:
800. 789. 8175
or Fax us back at:
516. 789. 3690

Name

Street

City   State

Zip/Postal Code   Phone

★ Send our free catalog of great Christian books to all your friends!

Name

Street

City   State

Zip/Postal Code   Phone

Name

Street

City   State

Zip/Postal Code   Phone

Calvary Press Publishing
Catalog Request Processing
P.O. Box 805
Amityville, NY 11701-0805

CHAPTER XII.

THOSE whom marriage, or other circumstances bring to a great city, often complain that everybody lets them alone. They come, perhaps, from a community where they have been known to all about them, persons of importance in their sphere, and are chilled and surprised to find themselves quite lost and unnoticed in the crowd they now enter. The truth is, there are any number of people in it just as good, just as nice, just as agreeable, as themselves, and unless they put on some badge that shall distinguish them from the rest, they will live unknown and die unlamented save by some very limited circle of their own. Now, is there such a badge? Yes, if you who feel lonely, unknown, isolated, will go about labelled ready for hard work, work will come to you, and with it congenial friends and co-workers. With no design save that of doing good, Maggie was entering warmly into the interest of the church to which Horace had

brought her ; she was always at the prayer-meeting, always at the sewing-circle, always at the mission school, always on hand when special cases
demanded special work. She talked little and did
much ; her early training fitted her for all sorts of
practical duty, and her habits of industry enabled
her to accomplish wonders ; and though she had
no money to give, she was becoming very necessary and very much beloved in a rich church where,
at first blush, one would say there was no lack of
service. It takes all sorts of stones, of all sizes and
shapes, to build the walls of a church : let no one
refuse to be one of those stones, however small,
misshappen, or ordinary he may be.

So, what with loving her husband and making a
bright, happy home for him, her class at mission
school, her little girls at the industrial school, her
sick child across the way, and many a deed done
by her right hand that her left hand never knew
anything about, "our Maggie" was one of the
busiest and one of the happiest little creatures to
be found anywhere. You could not tell why, when
she opened the door and came into a room, the
atmosphere at once grew sweet and fragrant ; why,
whenever you thought of her you wanted to take
her in your arms and kiss her ; nor why, if you
were in trouble you wanted to run and tell her all
about it. And those who only knew her as she was

now, would have found it hard to believe that it was not the hand of nature, but the hand of grace that had given her these subtle charms.

Yet all the sunshine that warmed you, and the love that satisfied you, and the sympathy that soothed you, were the reflection of His goodness and love and tenderness, with whom Maggie lived and walked. She was with Him so constantly, talked with Him so intimately, was so conscious of being at peace with Him, that her happiness flowed over its bounds and ran to encircle and gladden you.

Quarter-day had come and gone. At the very last moment Horace had been able to pay his rent, and that care was off his mind. But work was coming in upon him that made it necessary to give up most of his evenings to it, and this was hard for him and hard for Maggie, who, after longing for him all day, dreaded to see books and papers brought out to exclude her at night. But they were so happy in each other that they needed this discipline and that of their poverty, and unconsciously to themselves they profited by it.

One Monday morning Maggie had been unusually busy about her household tasks, and had not had time to put off her working dress, when a carriage drove up to the door, and Miss Fitzsimmons "that was," drawing her skirts daintily away from the dirty street, was announced, in an awe-stricken voice by Mary. For an instant Maggie's heart beat and her cheek flushed. Horace had honorably told her of his episode with that young lady, and she knew there was no point at which they should sympathize; and then her dress! It never occurred to her that she could go up stairs, deliberately take down her hair and re-arrange it, put on another dress, a couple of bracelets, an extra bow or two, etc., after the manner of not a few of her sex who think your precious time of no value provided they get themselves up in style. She went into the parlor, therefore, simply and frankly, met her aristocratic guest with true hospitality rather than furbelows, and was so perfect at ease that Miss Shoddy could neither put her down nor out of countenance.

"I have long been intending to call on you, Mrs. Wheeler, but my numerous engagements have hitherto prevented. I hope you will waive all ceremony and come to us on Friday evening; just a select party; a mere little social visit."

"We make very few visits," Maggie replied. "Mr. Wheeler can rarely spare an evening now; he brings his work home, however, and that makes it a little less lonely for me."

"I shall depend on you for Friday night, however. Tell Mr. Wheeler he must not forget his old friends. Though you are perhaps not aware on what intimate terms we were? Yes? Well, really I feel highly honored to find he has spoken of me to you. Good morning; remember me to him; Friday evening, at eight o'clock."

And then she swept out of the little parlor, and Maggie stood spell-bound for an instant, and then broke forth into a gay laugh that would have greatly scandalized the departed guest, had she heard it.

"I do hope Horace won't make me go," thought she. "I shouldn't like to say what I think of her. How dare such creatures call to see creatures like me?" And then she laughed again, and frisked back to her unfinished work more gayly than ever. Was this the laugh of contempt? By no means. It was the song of a bird that has soared high, and lingered long in an atmosphere far above this world.

"We shall have to go," said Horace, when Maggie told him of the invitation. "But she will soon drop us, never fear."

"But why must we go? We have no interest in common with such people. Why, all I can talk about is what we shall have for dinner when dinner is to be got without money, and what my Mission children are to wear, and what I am to teach them, and what they said to me last Sunday."

"Don't be absurd, child," said Horace, looking

7

at her flushed, pretty face with pride. "It will do them good to hear something from a world they never entered. What have you got to wear?"

"Will my black silk do?"

"No, indeed."

"She said it was to be a very social little party."

"Yes, that's the stereotyped word, but it means nothing at all. I remember my first entrance into fashionable life. The invitation was for seven o'clock, and the words *very socially* were underscored. Aunt Jane, who never goes to large parties, was deceived, as well as I, and as she chose to have me escort her, we reached the house not long after the appointed hour. Aunt Jane was very plainly dressed, and so were the very few guests we found there; but our hostess was all ablaze with diamonds, and threw everybody into the shade till two mortal hours had passed, when, lo! a host of birds of Paradise came flocking in, till the large rooms were crowded almost to suffocation. We got no supper till half-past eleven, by which time we were ready to sink with fatigue, and Aunt Jane took a vow never to make another 'social' visit during her natural life."

"And why can't we do the same?"

"Well, we are not elderly widows, and people would think us odd."

"Then let them think so. What do we care what they think?"

"But in this case we must go. Mrs. ——, what's her name?"

"Mrs. Read."

"Mrs. Read will fancy you are afraid to trust me in her charming presence, if we decline to go."

Maggie laughed lightly.

"Then suppose you go without me? I don't really think I've got anything that is fit for a regular party dress."

"Wear what you wore to Mrs. White's the evening we dined there. You looked so lovely then, Maggie."

"But I should have to get a pair of new gloves; and oh, Horace! we should not be able to walk, and if we took a carriage—"

"It would cost money. Yes, I know that, but just this once won't ruin us."

"No, but it will not end at this once, if we begin to go to large parties."

"What a nuisance it is to have to count every penny so!" said Horace.

"You really want to go, then?"

"I cannot say that exactly. But I must own that I should like to let that set of people see my little wife."

"If that is all, I will not go," said Maggie, de

cidedly. "Dear Horace, why can't we take a position of our own? we don't care for the world, and
it doesn't care for us; and we can't afford to keep
up with it either."

"Oh, to all intents and purposes, I have done
with the world," replied Horace; "but I rather
thought we ought to look into it now and then, if
only to make sure there is nothing in it we want,
and that we have nothing to give it. But if you
say so, we'll cut loose from it, and make a new one
for ourselves."

"Not for ourselves, but for everybody we can
help or comfort. Now that miserable rent is paid,
I'll tell you what I want to do."

"Well, my little woman, speak on, and speak
fast, for I've hard work before me to-night."

"I'll speak as slowly as I can," said Maggie, who
could be mischievous when she chose. "I want
to get up a nice little supper next Sunday night,
and have your Mission boys to tea."

"They wouldn't come."

"Leave that to me. I'll get round them. We'll
have them to tea; then we'll read a chapter; oh,
we'll read round, boys always like that, and have
prayers, and sing a little, and then I'll go down and
read to Mary in the kitchen, and you can talk to
them, and get at them as you can't do at school.
Then on the Sunday after I'll have my girls."

"And shall I have to go and stay with Mary?" asked Horace, demurely.

"No. After prayers you shall go and spend one hour with Aunt Jane. She misses the Sunday evening visits you used to make her after you were wounded, and I don't think you ought to give them up. I do not see how an own mother could have done more for you than she has done."

"If ever a man let himself be pulled about by the nose, I am that man," said Horace. "Well, get up your little suppers, and whatever else you like. Only now I really must attend to these papers. Kiss me, and let me go."

Which she did, but he wouldn't go. This little wife charmed him, he knew not why, and he did not feel like work after his long day at the office.

"I don't know," he said, untying at last the red tape that secured a roll of papers, "whether I most like or most love you."

"Was that remark addressed to those papers or to me?" asked Maggie, in a way that provoked the tossing of them all on the table, where they spent the rest of the evening untouched.

"I'll have stewed prunes for one thing," said Maggie, "and buns for another. Boys always like buns. And doughnuts. I wish we could afford to give them some oysters."

"We might, just for once," said Horace.

"But it isn't going to be for once," it is going to be ever so many times.   Well, I know what I'll have. There are plenty of good things that don't cost much, only they are not genteel.   But we don't set up to be genteel."

The next Sunday Maggie scared every boy in Horace's class with a tiny little note in which she called him "Dear Bob," or "Dear Jim," as the case might be, told him what she was going to have for supper, and coaxed him to bring his Bible, and surely come.

"Are you a-going, Bob?" quoth Jim.

"No, I ain't got anything to wear."

"I ain't either.   What do you suppose she wants of us?"

"To convert us, I guess."   Whereupon seven separate grins on as many separate faces.

"Cold suppers is prime," suggested Bill Rooney. "I'm a-going.   She knowed I'd come looking like sixty.   She saw me last Sunday, and she seen me this."

"If you're a-going, I am," said Bob.

"Let's all go," squealed little Tim Weaver, who never remembered having all he wanted to eat at any one time in his life.   "What's this at the end? Your 'aff.' friend.   I say, what kind of a friend is that?"

"It means that she'll be affronted if we don't

go," said Jim. "And the Cap'n says he wants us."

The thing ended in this wise. The door-bell rang at six o'clock, and the seven boys stamped into the house looking like seven prisoners about to be sentenced. There was a scuffle in the hall as to who should go into the parlor first, which was summarily ended by Jim's aiding little Tim's entrance by the skillful application of his foot to the small of his back, sending that young man into the august presence of "the Cap'n" and Maggie, with a jerk that took away his breath.

Seven hard faces looked up into Maggie's, and seven hard little fists were clasped by her loving hand; and then they got awkwardly into seven chairs, and looked as if they would like to run away. Bob had got on his elder brother's jacket, lent for the occasion, and was nearly buried alive in it. Jim had out-grown his jacket, which came only a little way below his arms, and girt him about like a belt. Little Tim could hardly walk, for he wore his mother's shoes, which fell off at every step, and even when he sat in his chair with his young legs dangling in the air; he blushed, and put them on, and they fell off, and were put on again, in spite of his loudly whispered admonition, " I say, you old shoes you, you'd better stay on, if you know what's good for you."

But now tea was ready, and Maggie got them around her little table somehow.

"Now, boys," she said, pleasantly, "we always shut our eyes and fold our hands, and ask God to bless our food before we taste it, and you'll do just as we do, I'm sure."

The seven pairs of eyes shut themselves together like a vice, and the rough hands were folded as in a mortal grip. Only little Tim couldn't help "peeking," as he afterwards confessed, to see whether all the promised things were on the table. Maggie had provided as she would have done for her own brothers, if she had seven of them, and was greatly surprised and disappointed to find how little these boys ate in proportion. There were various reasons for this. In the first place they were frightened half out of their wits. Then they had none of them the vigorous health of boys born of pure and healthy parents, nor had they been accustomed to the full meals to which the children of plenty are invited thrice every day. Still they had a certain pleasure in sitting at a well ordered table, and in drinking tea with "the Cap'n" and his dear little wife; and little Tim did full justice to all the good things, if the others did not. Indeed, he never heard the last of his feats on this occasion, as each of his comrades made an exact inventory of all he consumed, and never forgot

one of its items. The "reading round" at prayers proved an excruciating task to those who read
and to those who listened. Not one of the boys
read slowly or distinctly, or with a particle of life
and spirit; still, a chapter was got through, somehow, and then they all knelt down together while
Horace prayed for them as he had never done before. After this came the singing, and it was pleasant to hear the seven young voices reiterating,
"Yes, Jesus loves me!" over and over, till it did
seem that they must truly believe what they sang.
Ah, how little it was to Him what sort of uncouth,
ill-clad bodies held the souls he loved! Perhaps there was not in all the city a group over
which His heart yearned more tenderly than over
this.

Maggie skipped away after the singing, as she
had said she should, that Horace might talk freely
to his boys, and went down into the kitchen, but
Mary had gone to bed. So she sat by the fire
there, silently praying for each boy by name, and
that Horace might touch and gain their hearts,
and lead each one to Christ. At last she heard
them go shuffling out, and ran gladly up stairs
right into two arms that were waiting for her
there.

"They have enjoyed it, I am sure they have,"
said Horace, "and I don't know when I have had

7*

such a pleasant evening. How happy we are Maggie!"

"Yes, indeed," she cried. "No one on earth could be more so."

The next Sunday evening went off still better. The girls were not so shy as the boys had been; the true woman slumbered in each of them, and told them to sit at the table as Maggie did, not a foot from it; and after Horace had gone away, they clustered around their teacher with hugs and kisses and admiring glances, and let her talk to them as she pleased.

They were all clamorous to come again, and Maggie promised they should, for her heart yearned over them with love and pity.

Meanwhile, Horace was giving Aunt Jane an animated account of the evening with his boys, making her smile at one moment and filling her eyes with tears the next.

"You are forming just such a Christian home as I hoped you would," she said. "And you may depend upon it, that in blessing others you will find the richest blessing life can bring."

"It is all Maggie's doing," returned Horace. "I should never have thought of such a thing myself. Much less should I have believed that it could be such a fountain of pure joy."

"But it is not every man who would at once

have yielded to his Maggie's wishes," said Aunt
Jane. "I particularly like it in you, Horace, because you naturally like to lead."

"Oh, I lead now," he said, quickly. "Maggie
never sets up her will against mine."

Aunt Jane smiled. She could see the silken
cord of love by which Maggie was drawing him
along, and rejoiced in it.

"I wanted to see you alone," she went on, "to
tell you how very glad I am that you have conquered your reluctance to pray at our evening
meetings."

"That was Maggie's doing, too," he replied. "I
know I am not gifted in that line"—

"What is being gifted?" she interrupted.

"Why, one can't exactly define it, but surely
we all know what it means."

"If it means being far-fetched, and original and
striking, then I will allow that you are not. But
if it means really speaking to the Lord Jesus like
one used to it, in the language of simple love and
faith, without rhetoric or flourish or parade, then
dear Horace you are so far gifted that it is your
duty to lead us in our prayers whenever you are
asked."

"Thank you, Aunt Jane, you have taken a perfect load off my mind."

"But I want to take a mother's privilege and

suggest one thing, that it would not be amiss to do to every young man who prays in public. You all repeat the name of God too often, and if no friend has courage to tell you of it at the outset, the habit becomes fixed. I know it is a very delicate matter to criticise a prayer, but I do it in tenderest love, I might say pride. For when I think of what you were aiming at a few years ago, and what you love and are aiming at now, I could cry for joy."

"And so could I!" he said, while his eyes grew moist with grateful tears. "When I think of those days, days of perfect health and comparative freedom from care, for I had only myself to think of then, and these days when I suffer the inconvenience and privation of one limb less than I was born with, and the constant restriction of limited means, I am astonished at the superficial views of life that made me count getting into society a gain when it was only a sad, irreparable loss."

"God has been very good to you," she said, musingly.

"Yes. And what He has given me in Maggie, no tongue can tell. Why He should create and then give her to me, I cannot imagine. You don't know what she is."

"As I have not been married to her five months, perhaps I do not," she answered, with a smile. "But I have known her a great many years, and her happiness in you and yours in her does my old heart good. And now, before you go, let us kneel down and thank God for all He has given us, especially that He has given us Himself."

Well, it was not a "gifted prayer" that went up from his lips that night as Horace knelt side by side with his almost mother, but it told a story of love and faith that brought them very near to Christ and to each other, and sent him home a very happy man.

And there he found Maggie waiting to tell him all about her evening, with all sort of amusing things mixed up with the graver ones, and so ended a day that had had in it, and that had given to many others, some of the gladdest sunshine of life. Let those who do not believe it try it for themselves.

CHAPTER XIII.

THOUGH Maggie had once said there was nothing characteristic and individual about her new home, that could not be said now. For the sun shone on very few that were so poor, yet so rich; so strictly, often painfully, economical, yet so hospitable; so full of care, yet so free from care. Both Horace and Maggie had to trim their sails very closely; and those who know what it is to count the cost of every little item, know there is no poetry in that sort of life, that is to say, no poetry in the mere counting. Yet those who know nothing about these wearisome details, are ignorant, too, of many a little innocent joy born thereof, or rather born in spite of them. When Mr. Raynor, the great millionare, carried home to his wife one day a set of diamonds fit for a princess, she was proud and pleased, and on great occasions decked herself in them with no little state. But when Horace brought to Maggie a bunch of fragrant violets, with one or two words that sparkled with the love he offered with them, it is no exaggeration, *none whatever*, to say that this gift awakened more joy in her heart than her apparently more favored sister woman could be made to feel at any price. How often she had passed the poor girls and poor old women who sold these bouquets by the way-side, and refused herself the luxury of buying one; and now it had come to her fragrant with the love of the heart she loved best! And then, when after close consultation they went out together and bought some household treasure, long needed and at last attainable, how content they were and how astonished that five dollars could go so far!

Their identity with the Mission-school had given them good, estimable friends; there had been several simple entertainments given to the teachers which they had heartily enjoyed. And now spring had come, bringing among many other pleasant things a basket of eggs from Maggie's own hens at home, and her father and mother had come, too, for a little visit.

"We'll have all the mission and all the Sunday-school teachers some evening this week," said Maggie. "I want my father and mother to see how nice they are. Besides, we've visited ever so many of them."

"Yes," said Horace, a little dubiously. "Only

our rooms are so small. When I took this house,
I thought we should never undertake to entertain
visitors in it."

"You didn't know what sort of a Maggie you
were going to marry," she said, laughing at his
doubtful face. "I know what you are thinking of.
Oysters and ice cream. But I am not. I am going
to have cake and coffee; no more and no less.
The boys have sent eggs, and mother has brought
butter; I shall make the cake, and it will be sure to
be good."

"But nothing but cake and coffee?" said Horace.

"Yes, dear, what we can afford, not what we
can't. I am not ashamed that I can't get up splendid suppers; and I should be ashamed to ape the
style of those who do."

"What an independent little piece it is!" cried
Horace, going off to his office conquered, if not
convinced. Maggie wrote some of her invitations
and promised a pie to a boy who was kicking up
his heels in idleness across the street, if he would
deliver them; and ran round to see other friends
who lived near. Almost everybody came; everybody had a good time; everybody enjoyed the
cake and coffee and the agreeable host and sweet
little wife. But when there came signs of departure, Maggie went to Horace and whispered—

"We'll have prayers before they go, sha'n't we?"

"Oh, would you?"

"Yes, indeed, why not?"

"It will look so odd."

"Will it? But we don't care how it looks. It is the right way, I'm sure it is."

"Well."

And his momentary doubt and embarrassment gave way when a few minutes later he heard the voice of his Maggie's father in such a prayer as befitted a Christian home, where the Master of the feast was acknowledged as a welcome Guest. He was glad that he had this fearless wife, who was never ashamed of her flag, yet never paraded it; glad that he was under her gentle, loving guidance.

And Maggie, unconscious of this guidance, was glad she had such a good man for her husband, who always took such a decided stand on the right side! She enjoyed the visit of her father and mother with all her heart, and they enjoyed it with all theirs, as well they might.

"I want you to know, darling," her mother said, at parting, "that if anything should happen to us, your father and I should leave you without one anxious thought. We love Horace almost as well as we do you; he is a noble, true-hearted man."

These words fell sweetly on Maggie's ear.

"You can't think how kind he is to me," she said. "But it worries him that we have to pinch so.

It comes harder on him than on me, because I've always been used to it."

"It will not hurt either of you as long as you have health. And if that fails, God will provide for you in some way," said her father. "He is rich, and could give you more now if He saw that it would be good for you. Never forget that."

"I never do," said Maggie. "I would not have you think we are either of us discontented. But sometimes when we dine out, and I see the beautiful table linen and the delicate cut-glass and all the luxuries of that sort, it does shoot through me, —just *shoots* you know,—'Well, Maggie, wouldn't you like to indulge in such treasures?'"

"But such shots will not kill my little Maggie," said her mother, "nor even wound her very sorely."

"No; but I thought I ought to tell you that I am not an angel," said Maggie, laughing, yet with some feeling, "though I do want to be one."

"It would not take long nor be very hard work to turn her into one," her mother said, afterward, referring to this remark made in a sweet, shame-faced way.

"She is a chip of the old block!" was the reply, made in a tone that did the heart of the minister's wife good.

Maggie went home to spend the month of Au-

gust—Horace spending his Sundays with her.
She went to please her parents and the boys, rather than herself, for it grieved her to leave her husband hard at work and alone. And she did not
like to leave her scholars either; they loved her
so dearly, and she was getting such influence over
them. Still she had a happy month at the dear
old parsonage, saw all her old friends, said and did
a great many kind things, and wrote letters to
Horace that filled him with pride and joy.

So the first year of their married life was drawing to an end in a sunshiny way; Annie and her
Tom were expected home, and Aunt Jane had put
some business into the hands of Horace that promised to be very lucrative. They breathed more
freely, and Maggie promised herself the great joy
of doing more through the approaching winter,
for a set of poor folks she had in hand, than she
had done before.

As has been already observed, the house in
which they lived was in an obscure street, not far
from a number of tenement houses, wherein dwelt
swarms of ill-conditioned men, women and children, Whether owing to this fact or to some
other, about the middle of September Horace began to suffer with pains in his head, of which he
did not at first speak to Maggie. But she soon

perceived his flagging appetite and loss of strength and expressed her uneasiness.

"It is nothing but the heat," Horace declared. "I always find this early September weather trying; I shall be all right in a day or two."

But he grew worse rather than better, and the doctor, whom Maggie at last called in, uttered two words that completely disheartened her, for she had seen not a little typhus fever in her own village-home and dreaded it as those who dwell in cities dread the small-pox. And Horace so soon became unconscious of all about him that the floods of tears she shed did him no harm. She had never been a coward before; she had been a courageous, cheerful nurse, repeatedly, when there had been serious illness in her father's house. But now she cried day and night. The thought of having to live without Horace was so fearful that she found no spot on which to rest. She fancied his death, his funeral, her going back to live at home, and could have shrieked at the bare image. What sort of a home would it be? Why, the mountains that stood around it would lie before her like a dead plain; the fields and groves would be covered with a black pall forever more! And then she hung over Horace and begged him to speak to her once more, only once, and tell her he forgave the little faults which now loomed up before her imagination as so many crimes.

In this state Aunt Jane found her, when on her return to town on the 1st of October, she drove leisurely down to see them, ignorant of what was going on.

"My poor child, I didn't know you!" she said, taking the drooping figure in her arms. "Is this my courageous, is this my *Christian* Maggie?"

"Oh, I don't know who it is!" answered Maggie, and she went on crying in such a sorrowful, heart-breaking way, that notwithstanding Aunt Jane's tacit reproof, she began to cry, too, till neither of them had a tear left.

"Now, we shall feel better, and be able to talk," she said, smiling, and drawing Maggie closer. "Tell me all about it; tell me what makes you so hopeless."

Maggie told the whole story quietly, but pitifully.

"The hard part of it is that I can't pray," she added. "If I kneel down I just go to crying, and can't say a word; I know it is all right, and that I ought to be willing to let him go if God says so; but the bare thought of having to live without him makes me shiver."

"I do not want to try to make you fancy that it would not be a very grievous thing to give him up," said Aunt Jane, "but I want you to listen to what I am now about to say, because I mean a

great deal by it. Do you remember the story of
the sickness of David's child; how during those
seven days he fasted and wept and prayed, and
when he heard that it was dead, he arose from the
earth, and washed and anointed himself and changed
his apparel, and came into the house of the Lord,
and worshipped?"

"Yes, and it has puzzled me."

"But I understand it, and so do all who have
had a similar experience, or have observed it in
others. God does not give beforehand the grace
with which to bear His blows; He does not heal
before he smites. In your terror at the thought
of parting with Horace, you left entirely out of
account the sustaining power that would hold you
up and bear you through those awful moments;
you suffered in advance, and wholly in your own
strength. But how many, how many persons I
have heard say, I am a marvel to myself! This
blow, so long dreaded, has not slain me, as I ever
believed it would; I stagger under it, but I live to
wonder at the strength God gives me, and in which
I bear it. Just as the mass of people dread death
and declare that they shall shrink from it at last:
yet, for all that, the dying grace comes in the dying hour."

Maggie made no reply, but received these words
thoughtfully into her heart.

"Shall I go in now and see Horace?" asked Aunt Jane.

"If you are not afraid of taking the fever," said Maggie, and then wondered how she could use the word "afraid" to one who she well knew, understood not its meaning.

"What doctor have you?" was the next question as they stood together by the unconscious sufferer.

"Oh, I did not know whom to send for; you were away, and so was everybody I knew; I got the one who resides nearest, Dr. Page."

"I never heard of him. The next time he comes ask him if he is willing I should send my doctor, also."

They sat down together in silence, but it was silence before God. Then Aunt Jane said, "There is just one thing I want to say, if you can bear it, darling. Could you believe, if you did not know it, that out of a repulsive caterpillar there could emerge a bright-winged butterfly? But I want you to believe, because I *know* it is true, that joy emerges from sorrow, and soars on wings far more beautiful than any earthly analogy can paint. If God takes away your husband, He will give you something better in his place."

Maggie listened as we listen to a distant strain of music, not quite catching its refrain, not sure

whether it comes from heaven above or from the
earth beneath, yet soothed and quieted by it. And
then they talked no more, but sat watching the
day slowly depart, and if Maggie could not pray,
Aunt Jane could.

Yet though she loved Horace like a son, and
realized now how very dear he was, and knew, no
human soul knew better, all Maggie would have
to pass through if he were taken away, she did not
ask for his life.

"Thy will be done, Thy will be done!" was all
she said, or would have said, if every life that
beautified this earth to her lay trembling in the
balance.

But as night drew on she found her strength
failing, she was courageous and full of faith, but all
that does not turn a living, quivering human soul
into a stone. All her own past sorrows were re-
called by the scene before her, and the warm sym-
pathies that made her a comforter, re-acted sharply
upon both heart and brain.

"I shall have to go home," she said, "but I will
send some one to spend the night with you, and
to-morrow I will get a nurse. Don't open your
mouth on that point," she added, as she caught
Maggie's look of dismay. "This is one of those
emergencies when friends must stand by each
other: you must let me have the gratification of

doing for you and Horace what little extras his illness will require. You have been alone with him, and your cares too much as it is."

Maggie tried to smile her thanks, and did smile, but it was with a look that made Aunt Jane hasten down stairs into her carriage, and out of the way.

Meanwhile all was peace in the Stafford parsonage; Maggie had written once since Horace's illness, but not in a way to alarm her parents, for she knew they could not come to her. Could not, because it costs money to make journeys, and, except in a case of life or death, she might not send for them, they might not come, twice in one year. She had never felt the bitterness of poverty as she did now; yet she was too well acquainted with its trials to writhe under this new form of privation.

But three days later she found herself in the motherly arms she had yearned for, and that Aunt Jane felt she ought to have about her now that Horace lay just trembling between two worlds. For those three days had made his case look almost hopeless, and a few more such would bring the whole sad story to an end.

Maggie had ceased to hope; she had given him up, and wept no more. But none of the strength, none of the joy, of which Aunt Jane had spoken, had come to her, nor did she feel that she wanted either.

8

"Just to take the fever, and die too!" She said to her mother, "That's all I want."

"Are your father and mother, your sisters and your brothers really so little to you, my darling?" Mrs. Wyman asked, with such a pang as only a maternal heart can feel. "Everything is changed; everything is spoiled," was the mournful reply.

"Is God changed?"

"Oh, I don't know. I thought I loved Him, but now I can't love anybody. I feel like a hard stone."

"You are worn out, dear child," said Aunt Jane. "I wish I could see you cry as you did at first. Don't be bitter against yourself. If dear Horace goes, you will be the first to yield to God's will. But now you are physically exhausted, and even He is unreal. Believe me, believe me," she said earnestly, "you will get back to him; He will not leave you to suffer alone."

"She ought to go to bed and to sleep," said her mother, tearfully. "I never expected to live to see the time when this child, always so obedient and docile, would resist my will as she is doing now."

Something in these words went to Maggie's heart. She said in her sweetest way,—

"I did not know I was resisting your will, mother. Have you asked me to go to bed?"

"Yes, dear, over and over and over again."

"I did not hear it. Nothing gets into my head

now ; all people say flies over it.   I will do whatever you like."

Then they led her away thankfully ; this night
was to decide Horace's case, and they dreaded it
for her.   She fell asleep the moment her head
touched the cool pillow, and slept on, and on.
And as if he had only been waiting for this, Horace slept, too.   The nurse gave him stimulants
from hour to hour, rousing him for them with difficulty, and then they sat and watched again in silence.

Aunt Jane's physician came in the morning before he had had his breakfast.   Maggie had won
his heart by her tireless devotion to her husband.
After examining his patient he turned to the anxious faces studying his, and said, quietly,—

" He is saved."

There were a few moments of joyful tears, and
he then added,—

" When he wakes let him see no one but his
wife, and let her be perfectly quiet and natural, as
if nothing had happened."

" It is easy to prescibe," said Aunt Jane, through
her tears, and then she stole softly to tell Maggie.
After her long night's rest, Maggie was calm, even
peaceful.

" Do not be afraid to tell me the worst," she
said.   " I am ready for it now."

"I have come to tell the best," was the reply. And then she added the doctor's directions, Maggie rose, and dressed in silence.

"He is going to get well," she said to herself, "but this world is changed to me forever and forever. If there is such a thing as entire, absolute, uncompromising consecration to God, I will know what it means."

She went to her husband's side, and all the rest withdrew. What passed in her soul as she knelt there with his hand in hers, no human language can describe. Some would call it by one name and some by another; to all it would be, even if experienced, a great mystery.

At last he opened his eyes, and saw her.

"I have over slept, haven't I?" he said, trying to rise.

"No, darling; it is still early, go to sleep again," she said, steadily.

He kissed her, his feeble fingers closed a little over hers, just as they had done many a time when she had answered just so; she had got him back again; he was hers.

But was she his? Was everything going to fall back again into the old groove? We shall see.

CHAPTER XIV.

S that all you are going to give me? Why, Maggie, child, I am starving."

"That is all you'll get till twelve, no, till half-past twelve," replied Maggie, decidedly.

"At this rate I shall never leave my bed," said Horace. "How can you be so hard upon me?"

"I gave you a great spoonful more than the doctor said I might. Don't be unreasonable, Horace dear. You do not realize how very, very ill you have been."

"You have misunderstood the doctor, I have no doubt. I am not gaining in the least. How can I, fed on slops, like a baby, and fed by the teaspoonful at that."

Yes, this was the end of all her tears and sleepless nights; he was just as ungrateful, and just as unreasonable as a sick boy.

"I would like some water, at any rate. I suppose you don't begrudge me that. Don't look like an injured innocent, for pity's sake."

And as soon as she had given him the water and taken her seat, he wanted more light in the room, and when she rose, wearily, to let in more, he complained that her shoes creaked, though owing to this frequent complaint, she wore no shoes at all. And then he asked if it was not nearly twelve, when his next portion of beef-tea was due, and when she reminded him that it was to come at half-past twelve, he would fain have disputed with her on that point, only she would not keep up her side of the contest.

The truth is he was really more to be pitied now than during the days when he lay between life and death, belonging to neither. And fortunately for him, though Maggie had never had one sick day, she had seen enough of illness in others to know how to make allowances for him. What pained her was his apparent want of love for her. He never gave her a smile, or apologized for the trouble he cost her, or spoke in the old tender way. Once this would have nearly killed her, but now she took it patiently, biding her time, in full faith that he would become his real self as soon as his strength returned. Yes, and biding her time in a new life that had come to her she knew not how or when, but of which she was distinctly conscious.

It will be remembered that immediately on hearing that he was restored to her, she had mentally declared that she would consecrate herself to Christ as fully and as entirely as a human soul could do on earth. And this not from gratitude that his life was spared, but because of the terrible revelation his danger had made to her, of the strength of her love to him, and of the bondage in which she dwelt to it. She saw, as by a flash of lightning, that those who will love created beings as she loved, must have a love infinitely higher, unless they would sin and suffer infinitely; that she must give herself, not less to the husband of her youth, but more to her Saviour. And when she knelt by the bedside on the morning when hope for Horace first dawned upon her, a subtle, mysterious change passed over her soul. She went up into regions she had never traversed; came back to all the little homely details of the sick room, to tender ministrations, to loving cares and loving tones; Maggie, and yet not Maggie. If, as Horace slowly recovered, he found any change in her, it was one that gladdened and satisfied him; he had nothing to ask from her heart that it did not give. And yet she had passed out from a land of bondage; nothing could ever wring from her eyes such tears of anguish as she had shed for him; and she knew it. Perhaps such a change as this is usually gradual. But there is no reason why it should not be as sudden and as decisive as regeneration itself.

Unconsciously, not knowing what she said, Maggie let drop a word now and then, that let Aunt Jane see what had been going on within her. As she had not learned it from books, the Holy Spirit being her only teacher, she used the language of no school when she spoke of a sweet, soul-satisfying love to Christ that had come to her, as something new in her experience, but which she did not claim as anything rare or exceptional. Indeed, it had not come with observation, nor did it dispose so much to talk as to action. Every little deed was done now with a glad alacrity that created a sunshine wherever she went, and whereas she had been gentle and affectionate and charming before, there was now an added grace that made those who saw her day by day take note of her, not that she had been, but was with Jesus.

"Aunt Jane," said Horace, when he was beginning to be himself again, and was full of love and gratitude to every living thing, "did you ever see a more angelic creature than my Maggie?"

"I know of a word that describes her better and goes beyond yours," was the reply.

"Why, what word? But whatever it is it cannot do justice to the heavenly patience with which she put up with me when I was beginning to get well. I was like an old bear."

"Like a young bear, you mean. I really think an old one would have behaved better."

"Was I so very ill-natured? Maggie says she did not mind it."

"But she did. Be careful of her, Horace, for though she has always had good health, she is strung on delicate threads; I do not think it would take a great deal to break some of them."

"I will," he said, earnestly. "If anything should happen to her, I should not live a week."

"We never know what we can live through. It is not so easy to die as we fancy. And I think it is a great thing to learn to be willing and glad to live, after all that we rested and leaned on is gone."

Horace had not learned that lesson, nor did he feel like learning it. He lay back luxuriously in a delightful chair Aunt Jane had lent him—she was always lending it to somebody—and ate slowly, to make it last as long as possible, a bit of chicken Maggie had just brought to him, and which she had prepared with her own hands.

"How different this is from Mary's cooking," he said. "It is a good thing to have for one's wife an angel, who isn't above indulging one's whims when one is sick. Come here, darling! Are you sure

8*

it hasn't made your back ache, or anything, to stand over the fire getting up my dinner?"

" No," she said, laughing, " I am not at all sure. My back does ache and so does my head.   But I am going to have a cup of tea for lunch, with Aunt Jane, and then I shall be all right."

"All right!" responded Horace. "That's exactly what I said when I was first taken sick. Maggie, if you've gone and caught the fever, we'll both go off together, for I couldn't live a minute without you."

"Foolish boy!" she said, standing behind him, and soothing him with her hands as well as her words, "if I had been and gone and caught the fever, I should have been and gone and died long ago."

She spoke playfully, but those two who loved her so, felt great uneasiness; Horace looked at Aunt Jane, she glanced quickly at him, and their eyes met.

Maggie was really feeling very ill. But she kept up and kept about, and was full of sallies gay and sweet, that made them laugh in spite of her gradually increasing pallor. At last Horace, weakened and unmanned by his illness, broke into such a great flood of tears, that poor Aunt Jane could with difficulty restrain hers.

" She is going to have the fever, and if she does, she will certainly die!" he moaned.

"Hush, Horace!" said Maggie, dropping the tone she had assumed.

He stopped, like a frightened child, instantly.

"Listen to me, dear! I think I am going to be very sick. And I promise you that if I can get well, for your sake, I will. But if I can't—if I'm going, you'll let me go, won't you? You won't keep me back with crying and praying, from going to be with my—"

But she had been brave too long. Aunt Jane had only time to catch her in her arms before she was quite insensible; and Horace, too feeble to get out of his chair, could only look on, with groans that would have rent the heart of his little wife, could she have heard them.

She had the fever, there was no doubt about that, nor was it strange, after all the fatigue and anxiety she had undergone. Such things are happening every day, and nobody finds any fault with them till somebody puts them into a book. Then let that somebody beware! For books should not paint life as it really is, but as inexperienced young people think it ought to be.

Yes, our Maggie was very ill, and the same sorrowful scenes were to be rehearsed that had already been witnessed in that little home. A dispatch brought both Mr. and Mrs. Wyman to the sick room, prayers were offered in secret and in public, every kindness possible was shown, Maggie's little girls got together at the Mission and cried, and clung to each other, and the sick child across the street lay with a breaking heart upon her bed, and refused to be comforted. But Horace, helpless, lonely, bewildered cried and prayed and cried by turns; he had come to a full stop and gained strength no more. People said they had been lovely and pleasant in their lives, and that death would not divide them, and if one must go, it was well that the other should go too.

It was not that Maggie was so hopelessly ill, but that in her delirium she spoke so incessantly and lovingly of Christ, or rather spoke with Him as if already in his immediate and conscious presence, that everybody said she was on the wing, and all ready for heaven, too good, too saintly to be contented here, and that Horace ought not to keep her back by his prayers and tears, as they had heard she had feared he would. And yet something did keep her back; " she could not die," and did not. It is not true that as soon as human beings reach a certain point in the divine life, they are snatched out of this: saints move about us and among us every day. They live to be our examples; to be our dearly beloved and cherished ones; to remind us of heaven, whose spirit they have won: to pray for us and with us; to inspire and to cheer us. They are saints, but they see not the mark in their own foreheads; they wrestle with the powers of the air, and with their own spiritual infirmities; they err sometimes, and sin sometimes, though sorely against their will, but they are bearing right onward, and are more than conquerors through Him who hath loved them.

So Maggie came slowly back to the world where she was needed, and she and Horace entered once more the limited arena on which they were yet to fight the battle of life.

Both were changed. Both were more serious, yet more uniformly glad; they clung to each other more fondly, and yet with a joyful consciousness that whatever might now betide, their happiness could never be wrecked, for it rested not on one perishable life, but on a rock that has borne the shock of ages.

For Horace, if his experience had not been identical with that of Maggie, had learned that to love as an idolater is not to love as a Christian. And while he was full of thoughtful, tender services, and watched over her as he had never done before, and had entered into closer union with her than even that of the marriage tie, for there is no love like that which unites those who live to Christ, he knew, and she knew, that he was no longer a slave to her, as she was no longer a slave to him. The baptism of fire had purified their souls, and they had come out from it, hand in hand, and with songs to sing to other ears. It is true they were misjudged by those who had suffered less and learned less; but who has passed through this difficult, complex journey of life unassailed, and nobly understoood?

"That poor little Mrs. Wheeler has been at death's door, I hear," quoth Harriet Foot, sitting at table with her friend Georgiana. "He caught a fever in some of those dirty holes she had got him in the way of investigating, and came near dying, and then she took it from him, and came near dying too."

"Poor thing!" said Georgiana. "The last time I saw her she had on cotton gloves."

"They say," pursued Miss Harriet, "that she wanted to die, but Horace wouldn't let her."

"Wanted to die? Well!" cried Georgiana. "However, I don't wonder. They are so poor, and live in such small, mean ways. It was very selfish in him, I think, to get married when he was only making a living."

"It depends upon what he took her from," said Harriet.

"I've dropped them," continued Georgiana. "Of course she could not come into our set; I invited her once, but she did not come; was afraid to, I suppose; I merely asked her out of ceremony; I knew he would not let her come."

"But why couldn't she come into our set?" demanded her husband, who never lost a chance to take up, and set down, his glorious creature.

Georgiana vouchsafed no reply, but pretended not to hear.

"I suppose her sister, who married Tom White, will come into our set," he went on. "And of the two, Mrs. Wheeler is the prettier, and the more charming."

"Why, where can you have seen them?" cried Harriet.

"I saw them at my wedding, for one place," was the reply.

"At your wedding? Fie, you should have had eyes for no one save Georgy. Should he, Georgy?"

"It is of no consequence to me for whom he has eyes," replied Georgy.

"I was going to say," resumed Harriet, who was not particularly fond, now that it was an old story, of hearing these two quarrel together, "that those two creatures, Mr. Wheeler and his wife, are in love with each other to this day. While he was sick she nearly killed herself with watching him day and night."

"I declare, I am getting in love with the little

thing myself," Mr. Reed put in, casting a glance at his wife to see if this shot had reached her.

"And then when she came down with the fever, he did nothing but weep and wail week after week."

"Quite romantic!" said Georgiana. "You do pick up the nicest little dishes of gossip, Harriet."

"Oh, I could tell a deal more, if Mr. Reed were not present. The woman they had as nurse is nursing my sister now, and she heard the praying, and saw the crying and the kissing, and the dying embraces; such goings on! They must have been happy together, poor as they were, or they would not have made such a time at the idea of parting. It is a genuine case of love in a cottage."

"I hate such people," Georgiana declared. "They set themselves up to be better than the rest of the world, and are full of cant. It is such a pity after all, that I gave poor Horace the mitten. He is such a very handsome fellow, and I could have made something of him."

She looked triumphantly across the table at her husband, and met a look full of hatred, but he restrained the answer that trembled on his lips.

"Come, Harriet, we have idled long enough over our dessert," said Georgiana, rising. And when they had sailed off, leaving Mr. Reed to drink wine in moody loneliness, she added, "I do really wonder how out of all my admirers, I chose to settle down on Theodore. There were at least half a dozen that would have suited me better, if I had only known it. I had no idea that it made so very much difference when one married; had you?"

"You ought not to let yourself be so annoyed by Mr. Reed's little ways," said Harriet.

"You might as well say I ought not to allow mosquitoes to sting me," was the reply. "Theodore has got just enough sense to make me sick of him, and no more. But I suppose it's pretty much the way with married people after they get used to each other."

"I don't know," replied Harriet; "people don't tell tales out of school."

But the eloquent story of Maggie's nurse rang in her ears, and made her thoughtful for once in her life. As she had intimated, she had heard things too sacred to repeat, had had a glimpse into a world whose threshold she had never crossed. She was a silly, vain girl, but she had a heart capable of being aroused and touched. "I wish those Wheelers did not live in such an out-of-the-way place," she said, after an interval of silence. "I always admired him."

"And he always detested you!" cried Georgiana, venting her growing ill-humor on her dearest friend, as some people always do. "And at any rate, he is nothing to you now, if he is so desperately in love with his wife."

"That's just what I like in him."

"And it is just what I don't like in him, so let us talk about something else."

While this rambling conversation was going on, Horace and Maggie were sitting before their parlor fire. They were not yet well or strong, but it was a luxury, after the long weeks of illness, to be at last alone together and to talk over what each had suffered in the alarming, critical days of the other. Maggie's hand, white enough now, lay in her husband's, her head leaned on his shoulder; both were peacefully happy.

"Annie will be at home in a few days," she was saying. "I wish I had gained a little faster for her sake. She will be shocked to see her plump little Mag looking so thin. Couldn't you manage to puff me up and round me out, or stuff me with cotton, or something?"

Horace smiled and kissed the thin face as he had never done when it glowed with health and animation.

"I think," he said, "that something after the first meeting will shock Annie more than the effect of your illness."

"What can it be?" asked Maggie, lifting up her head.

" This house and the way in which we live. Annie's marriage to a rich man has changed her."

" Yes, I know, but nothing could quite spoil her. And when she sees how happy we are—"

" She will not see it."

" Why not?"

Horace did not like to reply, as he might have done, "she is incapable of seeing it," and yet he wanted to prepare Maggie to find Annie greatly altered.

He had detected in her letters a certain something that his own past worldliness made him quick to recognize, but which had apparently escaped Maggie.

" I hear a carriage at the door," he said, rising. " They may have come."

Maggie's color flew into her face; whatever else her illness had done, it had not made her heart cold, and the next moment she found herself in Annie's arms.

There was confusion and laughing and talking for a few moments, and then the sisters looked at each other curiously.

" How dreadfully ill you must have been!" cried Annie. " And Horace looks badly, too. It is a shame. But it is just your luck, Maggie. I always had all the good times, and you always had all the bad ones. Don't you remember, that it always happened that if any of the family were sick they took the opportunity when I was away and you were at home?"

And she laughed.

"You look just like a French fashion-plate," said Maggie; "I can't quite find my old Annie in these fine clothes, but I am sure she is in them somewhere."

"Of course she is. I hope you are strong enough to come and dine with me to-morrow. I've sent a dispatch to father and mother to come right on; we didn't want to go there at this time of year but of course I wanted to see them."

"And the boys?" asked Maggie."

"Oh, the boys are not coming In the hurry and flurry I forgot the boys. But they won't care."

"I am not strong enough to go out yet," said Maggie, "you will have to come here. Where are you staying?"

"At the Fifth Avenue. Tom didn't care to go to housekeeping, and as for me, after the easy life I've been leading, I'm sure I don't. Besides, we've only come home for a visit. We're going back again early in the spring."

"Oh, are you?" cried Maggie in a tone of great regret.

"Yes, we've nothing to do here, and may as well travel about and enjoy ourselves. Well, it is getting late, and I have not unpacked yet. I've brought lots of lovely things for you. Though I had the dresses made to fit me, and they'll hang on you like bags unless you make haste and fill up. Good-night, dear. I'll come down in the morning as early as I can; that won't be very early, for Tom is lazy and won't get up, and won't let me either. I'll be along about lunch time."

It was nothing that Annie had said that made Maggie fly to hide herself in her husband's arms as soon as she had gone; it was something in her manner that betrayed a preoccupied mind, a heart less loving than of old.

"Marriage always changes people, you know, dear," said Horace, soothingly.

"Yes; for the better or the worse," was the answer.

"And perhaps Annie find us changed; she may miss something in us that she used to find."

"But it isn't warm, sisterly love," said Maggie, trying, however, not to be sad. "And perhaps, after all, Annie will seem more like herself to-morrow."

"How shockingly Maggie looks, doesn't she?" asked Annie, driving off with Tom. "Did you ever see a creature so changed? All her pretty color gone, and her face so long and thin!"

"She looked very sweet, though, and was wonderfully glad to see you, as of course she would be. Horace has had a hard time of it, I could see that at a glance. I wonder how they would like a trip to Europe with us next Spring?"

"Oh, they wouldn't go at your expense, you may depend. Besides, your mother says they have grown so peculiar. We should not get on with them at all."

"They always were peculiarly delightful," said Tom. "I am sure I should have fallen in love with Maggie if I had not seen you first."

"It isn't nice in you to talk that way," said Annie. "Maggie wouldn't have looked at you if you had gone down on your bended knees. Sometimes I wish I was as good as she is, and sometimes I'm glad I'm not. I shouldn't have suited you at any rate if I had been one of the very pious, strict sort."

"Why not?"

"Well, after the way we've been going on since we were married, I wonder you have the face to ask such a question!" she cried, laughing. "Dear me, what would Maggie say, if she knew?"

"We've done nothing wrong. Nothing that everybody doesn't do who goes abroad."

"Have we behaved like saints?"

"Why no, not exactly!" Tom allowed.

"Well, Horace and Maggie have. You just get your mother to tell you about their poor folks, and their sick folks, and their prayer-meetings and their tea-parties; I declare I was afraid of them both and almost glad to get away. I have no doubt Maggie will preach me a regular sermon to-morrow. She had it on her tongue's end last night."

"Well," said Tom, "I was brought up among people that belong to the church, and all that sort of thing. And I always thought till I was married that such people were different from the rest of us."

"Of all the horrid things you ever said to me, this is the worst," said Annie, beginning to cry.

Tom protested that he meant no harm, kissed her, was ready to tear his hair to appease her. But she remained inconsolable. Coming home to Maggie and old associations had greatly stirred her; hearing of Maggie's life had sharply reproved her, and now her husband had said, by implication at least, that she was quite destitute of religion, and if she had often accused herself of that, she did not want to hear him say it.

"I was feeling badly enough before," she sobbed, "seeing Maggie looking as if a breath would blow her away, and now you've made me perfectly miserable. And I was so happy and had brought home such loads of pretty things, and thought we were going to have such a gay winter."

" So we will, dear," coaxed Tom.

Annie wept, however, till they reached the hotel, where she was consoled by a dainty little supper served in her own room, and then she looked over and tried on some of her finery and found it very becoming, which soothed her yet more. And Tom made amends for his unlucky speech by admiring and caressing her, and telling her how devotedly he loved her, so that her April-shower gave place to gratified smiles and condescending joyousness.

He lay awake some time that night wondering why his random speech had wounded Annie so. He had not made it with special reference to her, or with the most remote idea of giving her pain; it was one of his innocent blunders, such as he was continually making, he thought, and which she was continually overlooking. Then he reflected on the seedy character of Horace's coat, and the air of restriction about his house and home, and determined to do something handsome for him if he could.

CHAPTER XV.

THE two sisters, as they sat alone together at lunch on the following day, offered a strange contrast to each other. Annie's faultless dress gave her a certain lady-like air; she had taken pains to grow stylish-looking and, in a sense, she was so. Yet there was a little restlessness in her movements, and her face had lost some of its youthful brightness and freshness. Maggie's refinement, on the contrary, was all in her face and in the tone of her voice; she had no style, no manner, her dress was very simple, and everything about her spoke of an economy that in spite of itself had to be ungraceful. But she looked serene and satisfied, and when she spoke it was with a loving gentleness born of a very different world from that in which Annie had been living.

"I don't see but you are the same old sixpence!" Annie at last burst out in her old natural manner. "From what people say of you I fancied you were quite changed and spoiled. I almost expected to hear you begin to preach a sermon at me on

9 (193)

the pomps and vanities of life. But there you sit, eating like other mortals and looking as contented and happy as a queen."

"A great deal happier than any queen I know of," said Maggie.

"Is Horace good to you? I mean," she added, coloring a little, "is he what you hoped he would be when you married him?"

"Yes, indeed!" said Maggie, "all I have to complain of is that he spoils me so."

"Tom and I get on very well together, too," proceeded Annie. "For my part I like to be spoiled. And Tom has nothing to do, so why shouldn't he? He fairly loads me with pretty things, and then he admires everything I say and do."

"I hope, then, that you admire all he says and does!" cried Maggie. "Sometimes mutual admiration societies are good things."

"Oh, you know what Tom is—a big good-natured thing! I get out of patience with him twenty times a day, and then we kiss and make up. I never pretended to be as romantic as you are, or even as he is, but we get on together, as I said before."

"And are you really going back to Europe again?"

"Yes. You see mamma White would fain have

us come and live with her, but that doesn't suit me.
For though I can wind Tom about my finger in
anything else, when it comes to his mother he is
stiff. So, to put off the evil day, I am going to
make him take me back to Europe. After we've
traveled all we choose I mean to settle down somewhere and study!

"And *study!*" repeated Maggie.

"You need not look so confounded. I only
want to learn French enough to do shopping, and
Italian enough to sing with; you need not be
afraid of my turning into a book-worm. Tom has
helped me do my shopping thus far, but I don't
always want him watching every cent I spend.
Besides, it is mortifying to go about with other
ladies who rattle off their French as if they were
born to it, and to depend on one's husband to do
one's talking. And now, speaking of shopping, let
me show you what I've brought for you."

"Oh, Annie," said Maggie, trying to look pleased
at the display of finery, "how came you to spend
so much money for me?"

"What is money good for, as Tom says," was
the laughing answer.

"But these things are too costly for me, with
my plain ways; at least most of them are. Let
me keep the useful ones; they are just what I
need. You can't think how thankful I am for

them, they will fit me up for the winter. But this light silk dress, oh, Annie! I never go to parties; you must wear that yourself."

"You foolish child! Knowing what a little old maid you are, I had it made as simply as Mlle. Duria would consent to make it; and do you suppose I'm not going to have any visits from you this winter? This will be the very thing to wear when you come to dine with me."

Maggie yielded; it did not seem very likely now that she would go out to dine with Annie or any one else, she still felt so weak and disinclined to exertion.

"I am so glad for you, Annie dear," she said, when everything had been admired and discussed, "that Tom is so much under your influence. For I did tremble when you married him, lest being a worldly man, he would be a snare to you."

"Now it's coming!" thought Annie, coloring. "I don't see but Tom is as good as many people who pretend to be better," she replied. "He is as honorable and as generous as the day is long, and wouldn't take advantage of a fly. And he is as sweet-tempered and kind-hearted as you are, every bit of it. And you ought to see how good he is to his mother! By-the-by, to tell you a secret, mamma White always hoped he would take you instead of me."

"I was not in the market to be taken!" cried Maggie, with some spirit. And then she wished she had not said that; Tom was a dear, good fellow, why resent being selected for his spouse?

"Oh, I know nobody had the least chance after you met Horace," said Annie, gleefully. She had steered clear of Maggie's impending sermon, and delivered herself scornfully of the words, "Mamma White," and now it was time to go.

The weeks that followed were full of confusion; Mr. and Mrs. Wyman passing back and forth between the hotel and their rich (?) daughter, and Horace's house and their poor (?) daughter; Tom and Annie running in and out; display of dry goods, jewelry, pictures, infinite nothings; dinners, lunches, suppers. For a little time this pleasant excitement was good for Maggie, but it soon ceased to be pleasant. She loved her own quiet home, and the opportunities it gave her of doing good, and gradually resumed the habits broken in upon by her illness. She could not go to her mission-school yet, but she had her class come to her Sunday afternoons, taught them, prayed with them, persuaded them to pray, and was as happy as a human heart could be.

Horace was almost as well as ever, but that was not really well. He could not get exercise enough to keep up his health. The doctors said he ought to ride on horseback every day, but they might as well have said he ought to dissolve and eat pearls. He took care not to tell Maggie this, and she did not know how hard he found it always to take car or stage, when other men kept themselves young and vigorous by walking. Still she saw that he often was thoughtful, almost depressed, and asked herself if seeing Tom White and Annie so free from care, so able to put forth their hands and take whatever they would, was not, unconsciously, making his own poverty more conspicuous and painful. He was working hard, and working late; would he have to do this if he had no wife to encumber him? Pondering these questions, she, too, became more silent than was her wont, and Horace soon perceived and misunderstood it.

" Poor little thing !" he said, " I do not wonder she feels the contrast between Annie's lot and her own! Here she is sick and weak, and needing delicacies, and drives, and leisure, and I can not afford to give her enough of either! Ought I to have entered on this struggle, and to have let her enter it with me?"

"A penny for your thoughts!" said Maggie, coming behind him, and putting her cool hands on his forehead. He was sitting over some papers, but not occupied with them, and she saw that he looked troubled.

"Well, my dear," he said, "if I must confess, I was thinking of you."

"Of me! And with such a face?"

"Yes, of you. Think of Annie's position, and think of yours! And you are ten times as worthy of the good things of life as she is."

"Ah! I know what all this means. You think Tom and Annie happier than we are. Why, Horace, I am ashamed of you! We are the happiest people in the world."

"Are we?" with a comical look.

"Yes, we are. Only you get dyspeptic now and then for want of exercise, and then you get to thinking things. Come, now, if you could put everything back where it was before you knew me, when you had nobody but yourself to take care of, would you do it?"

"And go and board at a boarding-house? No, I wouldn't."

"Then hadn't we better put a good face on our little home, and enjoy it?"

"One can't always get into the mood to put on good faces."

"But one can bear the contrary mood patiently, and then it passes away, as moods will. Tell me one thing, are you over-working because of me?"

"I am not over-working because of anybody. Of course, if I had no family to care for, I should

work less than I do now, for lack of inspiration;
or, if I were rich, like Tom, I dare say I should
not work at all. I should fancy that I didn't feel
very well, and that idleness was my vocation."

"Then I'm glad you're not rich. I have been
thinking lately that God meant something when
he gave the work of dressing and keeping the garden of Eden to both Adam and Eve. He could
have made the garden take care of itself, or have
given all the work to Adam."

"Why, Maggie! don't you read your Bible more
carefully than that? He did give the keeping of
the garden to Adam, and to Eve he gave work that
Adam could not do, and which gave her plenty of
occupation."

"Well," said Maggie, drawing a long breath, "I
don't know how I came to make such a mistake,
but I have really felt troubled at your having to do
all the work, while I idle at home. For I certainly
thought God made Eve share Adam's labors in the
garden."

"I think that while I go on with my writing,
you had better refresh your memory by reading
the third chapter of Genesis. I believe I am a
little out of sorts, and have been looking at things
through the medium of a touch of indigestion.
Not a very glorious trophy to bring home from
the battle-field, is it?"

"It seems as if it was enough to lose one's limbs," said Maggie, "and not have one's health thrown into the bargain. Horace, dear, would exercise on horseback take the place of walking?"

"Yes; but then this beggar has no horse on which to ride," he said, laughing.

Maggie stood in thoughtful silence for some minutes, and then said in a low voice,

"*Now* I feel that we are poor. But this is God's choice for us; the choice of our best Friend. I am sure He could refuse us nothing that would give me the pain that the sense of your needing something you cannot have, gives me."

Her eyes were full of tears, yet she smiled as she went on.

"I don't know but it is a good thing to feel our own weakness; it makes God's strength seem so strong. We can't manage this business of your exercise, but He can, and I believe He will."

"Well, I feel all the better for this talk," said Horace. "You always build me up when I get down. And now, little woman, go about your business, and I will pitch into mine."

".It would be a relief," thought Maggie, as she sat down at his side with her work basket, "if I could talk this matter over with somebody. But if I tell Aunt Jane or Annie, that Horace needs a horse, or the use of one, it would be just the same

9*

as asking them to see that he has one. Oh, the money Annie spent for me in Paris! However, the hand of Providence guided hers; why should I fancy I could have guided it better?"

At this moment a note was handed her from Annie, which ran on this wise:

"DEAR MAG,—Tom has had to go and look after his mother, who must needs fall sick. And I have got such a cold that I can't go to see you or anybody. So jump into the carriage and come here this minute.

'NAN.'"

Maggie tossed this note to Horace, and ran to get ready. She knew he was too busy to miss her much, and it was pleasant to think of seeing Annie all by herself. Not that she did not love Tom, who treated her like a brother, but that his presence was some little restraint to her.

Annie came to meet her with unusual warmth.

"Just look at my nose!" cried she. "And this is the night of Mrs. Erskine's reception, and I wanted to go! Isn't it provoking? And a cold does make one feel so flat!"

"But you could not have gone without Tom."

"Oh, yes, I could! There are plenty of them who would be only too glad to escort me. But only think now, suppose Mamma W. should go and die! I should have to throw away all my lovely things, and put on black."

"Why will you belie yourself so, Annie? To hear you talk, one would think you had no heart."

"You wouldn't think so, for you know better. Do you know Tom and I came the nearest to a quarrel to-day that we have come yet. He wants me to go home to live, because his mother is out of health and out of spirits, and thinks it would cheer her to have us about the house. But let me show you how she looks." And Annie put on such a long, melancholy face, that Maggie could not help smiling.

"I think you ought to go if Tom wishes it," she said.

"I don't believe in mothers-in-law, much less in living with them."

"Nor do I, under ordinary circumstances. But with her only son gone, Mrs. White has no pleasure in keeping up her establishment. Think how lonely she is!"

"Well, when I married Tom, I thought I was going to have all sorts of good times."

"It seems to me you have almost all sorts. But was not your marriage to be for Tom's pleasure, as well as your's?"

Annie colored, and replied:

"I don't think it is very kind in you to take sides with Tom, and against me! If there is any one thing I always detested the thought of, it was marrying a man's mother and sisters. To be sure Tom has no sisters—I'm glad he hasn't—and his mother might be worse than she is. But if we go there, she will expect us to sit with her all our evenings, and make me go with her to her societies and things. And I don't like to be led round by other people, and never did."

"Just what we don't like is often just what is best for us, darling. *I did not like* to see my husband lying at the point of death, nor did he like to see me lying so. But I wish I could tell you what beautiful things grew up out of those unlikings. And as to being led about by other people; why, they are often God's hands. He is the real leader."

"Here comes Tom!" said Annie, in a tone of relief. She did not want to be led by God's hand; she fancied she knew what was good for her better than He did.

"How's your mammie?" she asked, as Tom drew near.

"Dreadfully low spirited. She says she needs some life and stir about the house. And I think she does."

Annie set her lips in a way that showed there

would have to be a fight before she should furnish
that life and stir, and then Maggie prepared to go.
Tom insisted on escorting her, and as they drove
off, asked, in a piteous way, what he should do to
pacify these two women, who, between them, were
bewildering him to the very last degree.

" I don't know what to make of Annie," said
Maggie. " She never used to be selfish."

" *Selfish!*" repeated Tom, in a tone of surprised
indignation. " My Annie ?"

Ah, well, what a mercy that love is blind !

" Yes ;" said Maggie, decidedly. " Your Annie,
my Annie, is not herself. But she is not spoiled.
I am sure that if she sees that you really wish her
to go home with you to your mother's, she will
yield."

" But I don't like to urge her so, and yet my
mother needs us ; I declare I never was so worried
in my life. There's nothing I wouldn't do for her,
and nothing I wouldn't do for Annie ; but I don't
seem to suit either of them," he said, plaintively.

" I am very sorry ; but I am sure it will all come
out right," said Maggie.

These words were simple enough, but they
meant a great deal ; she was sure that she was going to pray about this thing day and night, and
sure that God would hear and answer her in some
good way of His own. And though she did not

say this to Tom, he felt that there was significance in her tone and manner, and that she was on his side. He ran in for a moment to see Horace, and they had a little brotherly talk together, which did not amount to much in itself, but which led Tom to think, as he drove off,

" I do love that man !"

And made Horace say to Maggie, to her great satisfaction :

" The more I see of Tom, the more I like him. He is as good-hearted a fellow as the sun shines on."

" Aunt Jane always said so," replied Maggie, "and she has known him ever since he was a little boy.. But isn't it strange, that with such a good woman for his mother, he has grown up to be in and of the world ?"

" How good is she ?"

" Why, very good, I always supposed. She is the greatest hand for going to prayer-meetings, and societies and associations, and things of that sort."

" And who looked after Tom while she was off on these expeditions ?"

" Expeditions ? Do you call prayer-meetings expeditions ?"

" If they took her out of her house I do. Of course, I am not finding fault with them, but I

have observed that your burning and shining lights
abroad often neglect to shine as they ought at
home. And I know, for Tom has told me, that
coming home from school, and invariably finding
his mother out, he naturally sought for other society, and that not always of the best sort."

"But think how he loves her!"

"Yes; but that's something comparatively new.
It sprang up out of the death of his father.".

"How many good things spring up out of sad
ones!" said Maggie, thoughtfully. "Horace, I begin to believe that God distributes His favors far
more equally among men than we fancy. How
many poor people He makes rich; how many rich
people poor! Think how happy we are, and what
a little thing is poisoning Tom's peace, and Annie's."

And then she told him of her conversation with
them both.

"Well, I advise you to keep silent, and not mix
yourself up in the business. It is not our affair."

"I rather think I can leave it to the Lord," said
Maggie.

"And I rather think you must. You look very
tired."

"Annie grieves me. It hasn't been a good thing
for her to marry a rich man. I daresay my head
would have been turned just so, however."

"Yours, darling? What nonsense."

But he acted as if he liked such nonsense, and soon peace settled down upon the little household, and gathered them all under its wings.

But Tom and Annie sat far into the night, discussing the question his mother had brought to a point, the one coaxing, arguing, despairing, the other unreasonable, willful and blind.

"Very well!" cried Annie, at last. "It is plain that you care more for your mother than you do for me. To gratify her wishes you would sacrifice my happiness. If I had known you were such a man"—and she filled up her sentence with tears, adding, "It says in the Bible that a man should forsake father and mother, and cleave to his wife."

"Yes, it does. But mother repeated ever so many texts to prove that he ought not. It does seem as if there ought to be a right or a wrong to this question. Would you be willing to let some other impartial person, or persons, decide it? Horace, or Maggie, or both?"

"Oh, I can tell you beforehand what they would decide. They would preach sermons by the hour to prove that I ought to give up and let you have things your own way. I have no doubt they would find such a text as this in the Bible:

"'Annie, you naughty girl, do what your husband wishes!'"

In spite of her nose, which she had made even

redder by crying, Annie looked charming in her
husband's eyes, as she uttered these words in the
bright, arch way that always won him. He caught
her and kissed her, and said no body should tease
her, and that she was his own little pet, and—well,
they all talk alike.

And Annie hid her triumphant face on his shoulder, and knew herself victorious.

CHAPTER XVI.

MAGGIE was just going to sit down to take lunch by herself a few weeks later, when, after a furious ring at the door, Annie rushed in, threw herself into a chair, and burst into a passion of tears.

"What is it, darling? Tom?" asked Maggie, tenderly.

Annie shook her head.

"Then its mother—or father—or one of the children," said Maggie, turning pale.

"No, no, no; it's some horrid, horrid men that Tom went and endorsed for. And they've cheated us out of everything. We've got nothing left, not a red cent."

And Annie's tears flowed like rivers.

"Oh, is that all? I thought something had happened to Tom, or that mother was dead," said Maggie, with great relief.

"I should think you might say something to comfort me!" sobbed Annie. "To think that

Tom could be such a great big goose! It is just like him! He'd give away his head if he could."

"Dear Annie, it isn't half so dreadful as it seems," said Maggie. "Think now how good God is to take nothing but your money."

"You don't know what you're talking about," said Annie, impatiently. "Can't you think of something to say that will comfort me?"

"I wish I could, dear. If God had taken Tom and left you the money, would it have been better, do you think?"

"But why should He take either? Why couldn't He have let things go on as they were?"

"Ah, these are questions I can't answer, dear. But He knows why He does this or that Isn't it some comfort to think that He would not have allowed this to happen unless it was good for you and Tom?"

"How can it be good for us? Just fancy now, if you had put your foot down that you couldn't and wouldn't go to live with your mother-in-law, how you would feel to have things take such a turn that you'd got to go and live with her on charity? Such a letter as she has written me! I suppose it was too good a chance to heap coals of fire on my head to be thrown away. Just read that!" And Annie tossed a crumpled letter into Maggie's lap.

"It is a beautiful, Christian letter," said Maggie, as she returned it. "I wish Horace could see it. It would elevate Mrs. White in his opinion."

"He can see it, and welcome. Maggie Wyman, why don't you say something to comfort me, instead of magnifying Tom's mother. What have I done that I should be humbled and degraded into living on charity?"

"Annie," said Maggie, gently, "doesn't the loss of this money come as hard upon Tom as upon you?"

"I don't know. No, it doesn't. I had been poor all my life, and know just what I've got to come to; but Tom doesn't. He keeps saying he has got me, and that's enough. But he will sing another tune when he comes to sell off his horses, and wear shabby clothes, and all that."

"But you said you were to go and live with his mother."

"Yes, till we can get started on something. Tom says he's going to work. But what sort of work is he fit for? He doesn't know anything about business, and he is too old to study a profession, even if he knew enough, which he doesn't."

"I am very sorry for you both," said Maggie. "But by-and-by, when you get over this first shock, and begin to think how many things you have left, this loss will not seem so intolerable.

Oh, Annie! I have stood by what I believed to be my husband's dying bed, and have looked down into such an abyss of misery! And you may depend upon it that you and Tom may yet be happy together; perhaps happier than you have ever been."

She came and tried to make Annie lean her head upon her shoulder, but Annie drew herself away with a gesture of impatience.

So the hours wore away till it was time for dinner, when Horace came home, bringing Tom with him. They had been together all day examining papers, and looked tired and troubled. But as his eye fell upon his wife, Horace's face brightened; he knew he had come to a loving heart and a warm welcome. But Tom's face lengthened when he caught sight of Annie, who sat listlessly in a corner, and did not rise to meet him as he entered the room.

"Annie, darling," he whispered, "Horace has cheered and built me up so all day. Look up, and give me a smile, do!"

But she only burst into fresh tears.

They had a doleful time at dinner; Horace and Maggie tried to keep up some general conversation, but Annie was so dismal, and Tom so absorbed in her, that the whole scene was very awkward.

"I am going to stay here to-night," she proclaimed a little later. "I am too tired to go home. As for you, Tom, you can go to your mother's, if you like."

Tom's lips quivered. Wasn't it enough to become suddenly beggared, must his wife fail him too?

Horace looked on in silent indignation, Maggie with tears of shame.

"What can we do?" she whispered.

"Nothing just yet, dear."

"Mary," said Maggie, slipping down into the kitchen, "my sister and her husband are going to spend the night here. If you will run up and light the fire in their room. I will get it ready for them."

Now Mary, usually kind and considerate, saw fit to take this inauspicious moment to rise from her seat with a fling that declared her disapproval of this announcement. It was a little thing in itself, but it hurt Maggie as a blow would have hurt her; her pride rose at its injustice, and she was just going to say with great dignity:

"You are not to dictate whether I should have visitors or not!" when a better spirit whispered, "Hush, Maggie, hush; this is one of the occasions of which you have heard for being deaf, dumb, and blind."

So she went quietly away, Mary following noisily with the coal-scuttle, and her simple little guest-room soon began to glow in the cheerful light of the fire.

" I wonder what we can have for breakfast," she said, forcing herself to speak pleasantly, but Mary vouchsafed no reply. "Mary," she then said, "I did not tell you that my sister and her husband are in a great deal of trouble. And I know you always have a kind word or a kind deed for those who need it."

" It's very good you are to say so," said Mary, brightening. " I'll do the best I can for breakfast."

Mary was gained, and Maggie had conquered herself, so she went back to the parlor with a serene face, and she and Horace spent the evening in suggesting every source of consolation they could, except the one which for a time they knew neither Tom nor Annie would seek.

It was time for evening prayers. Horace took the Bible, and without apology or embarrassment, read a Psalm, and then he offered one of his simple, childlike prayers, taking Tom's and Annie's trouble straight to God, telling Him all about it, asking what they were to do now, and especially that they might have all the imperishable riches hidden in Christ Jesus.

Tom's tears fell fast; he had never thought of or cared for such riches, but he could not help feeling that Horace knew of what he spoke. And Annie ceased crying; the directness and simplicity of Horace's words, went to her heart, and for the time hushed it.

"On the whole, Tom, you may as well stay here to-night," she said, and Tom accepted the grace thus vouchsafed, with much gratitude and humility.

"Well," said Horace, with a sigh of relief, as they left the room. "Come here, my little wife, and let me tell you how I love you, and how I pity Tom."

This tacit reproach of Annie roused all Maggie's sisterly love.

"Don't be hard on Annie, dear," she pleaded. "When she gets over the shock, and comes to her senses, you'll see that there is more in her than you fancy. She is naturally energetic, and will fit herself to her altered circumstances, as soon as she realizes that she must. But I don't like the idea of their going and living on Tom's mother."

"Nor I. It is better for Tom to go to work, and carve his own way."

"But what can he do?"

"That I do not know. I think his mother may probably advance him a sufficient sum to start him in some way. He will, eventually, have all her property, you know."

" And then Annie will be rich again," sighed Maggie.

" Is there anything so dreadful in that thought?" asked Horace, laughing.

" It is not good for Annie to have every wish gratified, and to lead a gay life. It has turned her head and diverted her attention from everything but the mere outside, the mere shell."

" She has not been as happy as she fancied," returned Horace, " I remember full well how I fared when I tried to live in the world, and yet to keep on good terms with my own conscience."

" Why can't you tell her so? She likes you, and you have influence over her. She will let you say what she would not hear from me."

" I am thinking of it. What have we got for breakfast?"

" Now, don't trouble your poor old brains about breakfast!" cried Maggie. " After knocking about the world and living at hotels, neither Tom nor Annie care for anything grand."

In fact, when they all four sat together at Maggie's little round table, Tom enjoyed the novelty of its simplicity; his sorrows had not destroyed his appetite, and he was in really good spirits.

And then came morning prayers, and he found

10

himself elevated and touched as he had been on the previous evening. He was impelled by a spirit not his own, to whisper bashfully to Annie as he took leave preparatory to another day in Horace's office, "when we get a snug little home of our own, we'll have prayers, too, won't we?"

Annie started and colored.

Was such a proposition to come from him who had made no pretension to piety, while she, a member of the church, had never hinted at such a thing? She went to her room condemned and ashamed, realizing for the first time how she had been dishonoring Him whose name she bore.

She found Maggie making the bed.

"Dear me, don't do that child!" she exclaimed. "It is a pity, if brought up as I was, I couldn't do it. It was selfish in me to stay here last night; you've had to make a fire, and get your pretty little room all in confusion. But you and Horace have done us good, ever so much good, and I am not going to be so naughty again."

So they parted lovingly, and after Annie had gone, Maggie thought of many things she might have said vastly better than she had said. When Horace came home at night she begged him to go, after dinner, to see Annie. She thought Tom would be with his mother, who was still confined to the house, and that he could thus see her sister alone.

But Horace hesitated.

"I should not know what to say to her," he objected.

"God will tell you when you get there. And I will be praying all the while. I am sure Annie is a Christian, but marrying a man who was not, and leading such a distracted life, and having so much prosperity, has unsettled her. Think, dear, how happy you are since you came out decidedly on the right side."

"Do you know, darling, how much you have had to do with that?"

"I?" cried Maggie, astonished. "What can you mean?"

"I mean that I love you dearly, that's all," he answered, with a bright gleam like that of the time before the fever sobered him.

"Now you look like yourself again," she said, thankfully.

Horace found Annie alone, and very glad to see him, and they fell naturally and easily into the discourse he desired. He had a very straightforward manly way of doing things he found it difficult to do, so he said,—

"I have come to ask you to listen to a little egotistical talk; may I?"

"Why, certainly," she replied. "I always liked to hear you talk."

" Thank you. When I was quite a boy my mother persuaded me to join the church; I did it partly to please her, partly because I thought it was the right thing to do. I did not expect to gain or to lose much by this step, but I think now that I gained by it. For all through my college course it was a check to me; a disagreeable one, I will own; but still it kept me out of some gross vices. I read the Bible now and then, and prayed when it was perfectly convenient; and when my mother died, read more and prayed more, and amended my life in many ways. When I came to this city, I struggled into a set that I fancied represented good society; I followed their practices just as far as I dared, and if it had not been for Aunt Jane and my poor old father's prayers, should have given up even the outward semblance of piety. What little I had I concealed as carefully from the world about me as I should now conceal vices, if I had them."

" I have heard that you were much admired at that time," said Annie.

" I suppose I was, I certainly wanted to be. But there is not an element of real happiness in the world in which I dwelt. I had thoughtless gayety, but not one satisfied moment. Then came the war. That sobered me. I could not dance and sing songs and flirt with pretty girls, when my country was in peril, I enlisted as a private, rose rapidly, and then you know what happened next. It gave me something I had never had; time to think; and my thoughts were full of self-condemnation. Then as I lay upon my bed in the hospital, too tired to talk or to be talked to, I heard conversation between my good old father and Aunt Jane, that opened a new world to me. They spoke of the grateful joy in God, the blessed fruits of sorrow, the delight in prayer familiar to believers, in a way to inspire even a cold heart. At that time I had never known such joy; prayer had always been a task to me, and I had never tried to make my disappointments bear fruit. But now I lay there helpless, crippled for life, weak in body and weak in soul; mourning for my lost limb as a mother mourns for her child, finding support and comfort in nothing that was left to me. It was then I turned heart-sick to God in a way quite new to me; and I can tell you, Annie, that he who seeks Him halt and maimed does it with cries of anguish that reach His ear."

" I had no idea that you felt, that any one felt so," said Annie. " I never realized that to lose a limb was so terrible. I have often laughed and joked about such things. But I never will again."

" I came back here a changed man," continued Horace. " But old associations still had power

over me; I did not take the open, manly stand I
might have done. *I was ashamed of Jesus* when
with those who despised and forgot him. I wanted
to get His sympathy with me in my trials, but I
wanted to do as Nicodemus did, visit Him by
night. But Maggie broke in upon that cowardice,
and led me, step by step into open acknowledg-
ment of His claims. But still I served Him a good
deal as a slave does his master, and when I prayed,
instead of finding the delight I had heard de-
scribed, I felt as one does who throws missiles into
an enemy's camp. But see how good He was.
He came and threw me once more upon a bed of
pain, made me feel as if I never should lift hand or
foot again, and then when I was beginning to get
well and to snatch at the world again, He threat-
ened to take away my Maggie. This time he broke
my heart all to pieces, and then showed me what
he could be to such a heart. This world was
greatly changed to me before our illness; now it
is quite a new one."

"But you seem cheerful, you seem happy," said
Annie.

"I hope so, for I am one of the happiest men on
earth. I am not now afraid of evil tidings or of
misfortune in any shape. I have endured, in imagination, it is true, but still I have endured, the
loss of my precious wife, and have learned that in

love and faith I could bear even that crowning
sorrow. And now, dear Annie, you will see that
having given the world a fair trial, I am justified
in speaking earnestly of its imbecility in the su-
preme hours of life ; and having tried God, I am
justified in giving my testimony to His power to
console the saddest heart."

"All you say is true, I dare say," said Annie.
"But I don't feel it. I had a real good time in
Europe, and after we got back. If things could
have gone on just so, I should not have asked for
anything better."

"Ah, but it is not in the order of life for things
always to go on just to our minds. That is the
very point. If they did, we should never ask for
anything better. That is just our folly and blind-
ness."

"After all you have said I have no doubt that if
I could find a world without any trouble, I should
go and live in it."

"There is such a world."

"Yes, but we can't go to it at any moment we
are tired of this. There would be a great rush if
we could."

"And do you really believe that if you went to
it just to escape the troubles of this life you would
be happy there ?"

"Why not ? The Bible says so."

The Bible says that the great employment of heaven is praising God. Now, suppose a crowd of people dissatisfied with what He has done with them here, rush there on that account, would His will be any sweeter to them than it was before, and would they burst forth into songs of praise?"

" Why, Horace, what a good preacher you are," cried Annie, " I had no idea you were up to it."

Horace, full of enthusiasm, sure that he should gain Annie in a single evening, felt as if he had wasted it as these words fell on his ear.

He looked at his watch, and found that it was time to go.

" I am a poor bungler," he said, "and sometimes wonder how I ever dare to try to do any of my Master's work.   But we felt so sorry for you, Maggie and I."

And then he went away.

But Annie sat and pondered his words long after he had gone ; she could hardly believe that Horace usually bright even to gayety, had uttered such serious ones.

" I suppose he is right," she said, with a sigh, " but I never did like your really good people."

And she would not listen to Him whose Holy Spirit spake within her.

CHAPTER XVII.

EANWHILE Tom, finding his mother tired and indisposed to talk, had stepped in for a minute, as he thought, to speak with Maggie.

"How cosy you look here," he said, welcomed by a bright fire and a glad face. "After all if people only thought so, they could get along with far less than they do. Where is Horace?"

"He has gone to see Annie. I thought he could say something to comfort her. But there is little one can do for friends in trouble."

"I don't know about that. I do not believe you realize what a comfort your sympathy has been to us. You have been like an own brother and sister."

"That's just what we want to be to everybody who needs us."

"It is a little peculiar, isn't it? Most young folks get out of the way of long faces, if they can."

"But your's hasn't been long."

"Hasn't it? Maggie, I'll tell you what I've been

10*   (225)

thinking. I want to turn over a new leaf, and live as you and Horace do."

"Really?" cried Maggie, joyfully. "Have you told Annie?"

"Not exactly. You see it is not so easy to break up old habits. Not that I've been doing anything so very bad. But still I know there's a vast difference between being moral and being religious."

"What shall I say to him?" was Maggie's silent prayer before she replied.

"If the loss of your fortune gains Christ for you, it will be a beautiful loss."

There was a pause, and then she said: "Did you ever hear of a rich man's going around to this and that friend, begging him to spend his life in trying to become rich, hardly taking time to count over his own gains in his eagerness for the welfare of others?"

"Why, no, I never did."

"But those who know the most about the riches Christ gives, can hardly keep their hands off those they meet, they are so much in earnest about seeing His heirs enter into possession."

"Do you feel so?"

"Yes, I do."

"Towards me?"

"Yes, Tom, towards you," she said, her eyes filling with tears.

His eyes filled too.

"I knew somebody was after me," he said, with increased embarrassment, "but I thought it was only my mother."

"It was your mother and my mother and father, and Aunt Jane and Horace, and maybe your little sister Maggie."

"Well, I am not going to stand out against such prayers. I'm as ignorant as a heathen, and somebody will have a hard time pulling me along. But if you and Horace will help me, I will begin."

"To begin what, dear Tom?"

"To be good."

"But you can't be good, and we can't help you to be. All you've got to do you can do now, sitting on that chair."

"And what is that?"

"Give yourself to Christ. Then ask Him to give you repentance and faith, and everything else you need."

"But I thought it took a long time, and that people had to read and pray, and get wretched, and then at last they would feel their sins roll off their backs in a great bundle, and go on ever after relieved."

"But that is not true. The first thing is to believe in Christ, and give yourself to Him, sins and all. I dare say that you will want to shut yourself up to thank God for accepting your gift, and to read the Bible and to pray; but as to wretchedness, I do not see where there is any room for that to come in. Oh, Tom, it is such a blessed thing to love Christ and to belong to him."

" I've been thinking so ever since we came home and got well acquainted with you and Horace. But we lived in a good deal of a whirl, and I never talked to any one as I have to you; I don't know how it has happened. And as for Annie—"

"Annie will come out all right," said Maggie. " She has had her head turned for a time, but she is not the only person to whom that has happened. If you take her to your mother's she will come at once under her influence, or if you have a little home of your own, gay friends will soon drop you, and you can live as you please."

" Annie does not like my mother. I never could see why. She is a dear, good mother, and loves Annie like an own daughter."

" Annie is very independent, and she is afraid of not having full liberty if she lives with your mother. But you will see that she will become another creature sooner or later. I have known her longer than you, and I know what she was before you began to flatter and to spoil her, and to give her everything she wanted. You nave never seen her best side."

"Maggie," he asked, abruptly, "doesn't it say
in the Bible that you must repent and believe?
But you say believe and repent. Now, I do believe, I am sure I do; but when I try to realize
that I am a great sinner, I can't, and am as hard
and cold as a stone."

"I don't think the Bible lays down laws about
the order in which God shall grant us His gifts.
To one He gives repentance first, and faith and
love afterward; to another, faith and love, and
they lead to repentance. The more we love Him
the more we see how sinful sin is, and the more
sorry we are to have been guilty of it."

"Do you think, then, that I am, perhaps, one
who loves God, and may get repentance for the
asking?"

"Yes, I do. One man enters the kingdom with
an intelligent sense of past wrong-doing, and He
who came to save from sin becomes the door to it.
Another enters, unconscious to a degree of his
unworthiness, and is drawn by cords of love, and
He who loves those who love Him becomes his
door. I know more about these diversities by
hearing my father speak of them, than I could do
from my own observation, and he always says to
those who seek the way of life through Christ,
'Come in, ye blessed of the Lord!' whether they
come weeping or smiling. Once in His kingdom

He will rectify their mistakes, give courage to the
timid, strength to the weak, wisdom to the ignorant, and penitence and love and faith to all.   You
will fancy it presuming in me to take this ground,
but if I had taken it years ago it would have saved
me much needless pain.   I thought I must force
myself to dreadful agonies of repentance.   At last
it came to me that all I had to do was to believe,
and that Christ would give me all else that I needed.
And I've been a great beggar ever since."

"And would you have me do that?"

"I would have you go home to-night and say to
Annie, 'God has given me a little faith, enough to
make me want to tell you of it, and I am going to
pray to Him day and night till He gives me all He
has to give.'"

"But suppose when I get up to-morrow morning, I feel that no change has taken place in me?"

"I will not suppose any such thing.   If you get
far enough to say that to Annie, you'll get farther."

"I'll say it," he returned.   "And if it ends in
my becoming a Christian man, that will be your
doing, Maggie.   I've tried to be one again and
again, but always wound up at the want of feeling
right."

He went away and said the lesson Maggie had
taught him, like a simple-hearted, obedient boy;
and added, "Are you glad, darling?"

"Yes," she said, ready to choke, "I am."

"It will be just like his love to his mother," she said to herself, long after he had fallen asleep. "It will not make any difference how I think and feel; he will do whatever he fancies right. And if he starts under Horace and Maggie, I may as well say good-bye to this world at once. And I do not believe in that. It was made for us to live in and to enjoy. Good people do enjoy it, and expect to go to heaven just the same. Mr. and Mrs. Jay go to the theatre regularly, and they belong to the church. Mrs. Bridges goes to balls, and dances round dances, but she is good, and gives away loads of money to the poor. And there's Henrietta Page! she is strict about going to the prayer-meeting, and reads her Bible, and has a class in the Mission-school, but she indulges in all the public entertainments, and dresses like a princess; but she expects to go heaven for all that."

"Will she enjoy heaven?" whispered a voice that seemed to be a re-echo of that of Horace.

"I suppose so. I suppose we all shall. I never did believe that some few saints had a right to lay down laws for every body else. If they like to sing Psalms and go to meeting better than any thing else, why let them; who cares? But why should they force their likings on to us young folks? I want to go heaven, but I want to enjoy

myself while I'm here, and what is more, I will.
Of course I am a Christian; if not, father would
not have let me join the church; and, of course, I
want to be good, and mean to be; but to wear a
long face and look solemn—what did you say? Does
Maggie? Why, no, I can't say she does, but most
of her set do; or at least I should think they would,
for they never do anything but visit the poor and
the sick, and go to meeting, and all that. I wonder if I had given more to the poor, whether God
would have taken away all our money so? Now,
just hear Tom! He is breathing away as peacefully as a little baby, and yet he has lost such a fortune! He little knows what is before him."

Thus musing, Annie grew feverish and sleepless.
Everything looked gloomy and hopeless as she lay
there alone in the darkness. Worst of all an un-
easy conscience kept her close company. She
knew perfectly well that she had not lived up to
the vows she had made to God, and that she had
taken for her standard not those who loved and
served Him best, but those who gave him nig-
gardly gifts from selfish, worldly hearts. But there
is really but one true standard, and that is not the
life and doctrines of any man or woman on earth.
The Bible is our only rule of faith and practice.
If that tells us that our chief end on earth is to
make ourselves comfortable, why we need have no

misgivings in doing so. But if, on the contrary, it utters such words as these, "She that liveth in pleasure is dead while she liveth," and calls for self-denial and promises tribulation, it follows that we have something to do in this world beyond seeking mere pastime and amusement. Do these words sound like words of gloom? Ah, then, let us read on, and hear its songs of joy and its hymns of praise; what it promises to give and what it has given. Those who accuse the saints of being too saintly, forget that not even the saints originated God's word, but that "holy men of God spake as they were moved by the Holy Ghost."

"What are you doing, Tom?" asked Annie, when she awoke.

"I am reading," he said, coming forward with a book in his hand.

"That's something new," she said.

"Yes, everything is new. Just hear this: I think it is beautiful. 'In the world you shall have tribulation, but fear not, I have overcome the world.' I suppose I have read that before, but it has come to me this morning as something strange."

"Tom, do you feel well?" asked Annie, abruptly.

"Perfectly well; why not?"

"I didn't know but you were going to die, you're getting good so fast."

"Good? Oh Annie, I wish I were! But I begin to think that I have done nothing all my life but do everything I ought not. Did you ever feel so?" he asked, with great simplicity.

"I am not a doctor of divinity," said Annie, wearily. "Don't you see that I have the headache, and do not feel like talking?"

Tom was instantly all concern and tenderness, and Annie's undefined, jealous fear that she was losing him, gave way before the pleasant sense of possession.

"I am such a bad old girl," she said, at last, "that I was afraid your getting good would make you care less for me. And indeed, Tom, that wouldn't be fair, for I've been the making of you. You always were good natured and kind; but you wasn't a bit bright, and I took you and woke you up. Everybody says so."

"I know it, darling. And then Maggie woke me up again; or rather Horace and Maggie did, between them."

Annie had always felt herself to be greatly Tom's superior, but when, after she had risen and breakfasted, he said to her:

"If you won't criticize your poor old husband, we'll read a chapter and pray together before I go down town," she was perfectly overawed. She had not aroused that simple but sluggish nature to do this, not she! God's Spirit alone could have emboldened him, whom she had led about as her great plaything, to take the dignified position to which she should long since have pointed him. And when she heard him pray—him, her Tom— her pride broke down and she burst into bitter, passionate tears.

Nothing could be gained by a description of the weeks that followed. Tom had come into God's kingdom like a simple, single-hearted child. But her return to Him after careless, thoughtless, prayerless living, was painful and wearisome. Many a time she would have faltered but for the Christian friends who rallied around her with their prayers, their sweet counsels and their faith.

"Oh, Tom, how good God was when he took away my great snare!" she said, at last, when the conflict was over and peace had come in like a flood. "I was not fit for prosperity, and He knew it. He humbled my pride, and made you my teacher! I could not have believed I should ever sit at your feet; but I do; you know more than I do, and I hope you always will!"

Poor Tom! he was six feet high and well built, but when she talked so he felt that he could creep into a nut shell.

They had left the hotel and its very dangerous temptations, and at Annie's own request had come to his mother's. For the present, at least, it was the best thing they could do, and to Tom it was in every way agreeable. But Annie went because she was beginning to live less in herself and more in others, and at first it was very irksome to her to be dependent on one whom she had recently sneered at as "one of your prayer-meeting women." But Tom soon found employment, and it proved to be pleasant after the useless life he had led, and he and Annie often discussed the question of setting up a little home of their own. But Mrs. White always had some reason for deferring this, and so they kept staying on.

Horace lost no time, meanwhile, in impressing into his service these two young people whose cooperation with him in his Mission work was so timely. He gave to Annie a class composed of its very worst boys. Her quaint bright words soon secured their attention, they would listen to her when they would let no one else come near them, not even Maggie. And then, in imitation of Maggie, she had them to tea and amused and interested them in ingenious, original ways, such as would have entered no other head save hers.

"She is a strange, bright bird," Mrs. White confided to Aunt Jane. "I never saw anybody like her. She flies into a room on wings, lights down where she will, but always in the right place, sings as she flies, and never seems to have a care."

"Don't try to turn her into a little white chicken," said Aunt Jane. "She is one by herself, and must fly where others walk. She seems to me now very much as she did when I knew her as a little girl, full of sunshine, running over with the joy of the moment, glad to be alive. She has vitality enough to make three or four enthusiastic girls."

"Oh, I love her," said Mrs. White. "Only sometimes her odd, imprudent words and songs come back and startle me."

"It will not hurt you to be startled," was the cool reply. "Let my bright bird alone."

And the bird did flit and flutter at first, but after a while found her right place for a bird of plumage just as bright as her own, flew from under her wings and put the whole household into a perfect flood of surprise and delight.

Annie could not be exactly like anybody but herself, nor could her baby; but they both created a new life in a home that had long been too silent, and Mrs. White's health came back as she forgot her ailments in rapturous contemplation of the little stranger.

Of course it was not a common baby. Annie said it wasn't, and Tom said it wasn't, and Horace and Maggie and Mr. and Mrs. Wyman all said the same. And the baby accepted the situation with dignity. And when they all called her their cherub, their rose, their bird of paradise, she smiled with the calm content of one who had long since heard those musical words and learned them all by heart.

But while Annie sang glad songs and talked gay talk to her baby, it was not out of the thoughtless heart of past days. It had been stirred to its depths by remorse, by penitence, by suffering and by joy. She had come out of darkness into a great light; a light that was to shine more and more unto the perfect day, and to serve as a beacon for many a tempest-tossed soul that would never have otherwise reached the haven where it would be at rest.

Ah, there must be all sorts of lights on the shores of time! There must be the moonlight radiance that never flickers or goes out; the great glow of the noon-day sun, the twinkle of the stars, the erratic shoot of the signal-fire. They shall differ from one another in glory, , but each shall have its appointed work and do it well, nor can one do the work of the other or shine as to itself.

CHAPTER XVIII.

E come now to the autumn of 1866. Horace and Maggie have been buffeting the waves and breathing the fragrant gales of three years of married life.

"How shall we celebrate our wedding-day?" Maggie is asking Horace. "Shall we have Tom and Annie and the baby to dinner, or go to Aunt Jane's?"

"Has she invited us?"

"Yes; here is her dear little note. I fancy her poor old hand is growing a little tremulous."

"We'll go there, then; that is, if you say so."

"But it is Annie's wedding-day, too, you know. However, Aunt Jane has invited her of course."

"Perhaps we had better go there. It certainly is a good thing to break in on the routine of one's life occasionally."

"Is our's a life of routine?" asked Maggie, surprised at his tone.

"I will not answer for yours, but mine certainly

is. I go to the office at just such an hour, drone
through a certain amount of work, step out for my
lunch, go to work again, come home—ah, the routine stops there, I will own. You always contrive
to have something pleasant for me, if it is nothing
more than running to bid me welcome."

"Still, it is plain you feel the monotony of your
life to be painful. Well, sometimes I feel mine to
be. To get up every morning and go through a
series of forms preparatory to making one's self
presentable, thinking how short a day will inter-
vene before these forms will have to be gone
through with again in a reverse way, is sometimes
a little oppressive. But is there not a story of a
wedded pair who changed places with each other
one day because of this sort of discontent? The
man staid in the house and cooked the dinner and
rocked the cradle and mended the stockings; the
woman went into the field and ploughed, and fed
and watered the cattle and the like. And that
day's experiment sufficed for a lifetime."

"I think I can get started for the day on that
story," he said. "I feel no drawings toward cooking of dinners or mending of stockings. As to
rocking the cradle, ah Maggie, perhaps we should
quarrel over that if we had one."

"Yes, I can fancy that you would take to that
sort of work you are so fond of your little niece.

But if God does not give us children, knowing as He does how thankful we should be for them, it is surely because He has some good reason for it. Perhaps there are now in the world some fatherless and motherless little ones that He is saving for us till we can afford to take them in."

After he had gone Maggie stood for some moments just where he had left her, lost in thought, and with a shadow on her face. He had touched on a very sore spot when he had hinted that this childless home was a disappointment to him.

For if it was such to him, what was it to her? She had never known until her marriage what it was to live without the sweet self-denials that are born of the helplessness of childhood; she missed the sound of little feet, the caresses of little arms. Home-life was preëminently the life she loved best; it was her instinct to hide in retired nooks, and if she reigned anywhere, to reign in a small, unobtrusive domain. But now she had health and leisure, and rather than be idle in God's vineyard she would work in more conspicuous, less congenial ways. Only there was Annie, so bright, so free from the shyness that makes outside duty painful, so fitted to adorn almost any sphere, tied down to a baby who would have loved some other mother just as well, and whom she, Maggie, would have been so much gladder to possess. For Annie disliked babies in general, while, of course, loving her own in particular; and the details of the nursery were as distasteful to her as they were an enthusiasm to the heroine of the doll-dressing witnessed years ago by Horace.

Yes, there was a shadow on Maggie's face, and there were tears in her eyes; Horace would always have to find his happiness chiefly in his home, walking was so irksome and painful to him, and what is a home without children? She had felt often before, and she felt now for his sake, like uttering the passionate cry:

" Give me children, or else I die!"

She crept away to her own room in this strangely stirred mood, and told her story to Him to whom she always told everything that perplexed, or pained or gladdened her. And then she said He should give or withhold, just as He pleased; that she would not plan or choose for herself; that she loved Him and believed in Him, and was satisfied and happy in Him. She might well say that, for the sweet throwing away her own will that she might take up and bear His, brought with it a peace and a joy that all the united treasures on earth could not have bought. Horace saw it in her face when he came home to take her to Aunt Jane's, and loved her forit, without knowing at exactly what spring she had been drinking.

And Aunt Jane saw it too, and felt it in the unusually fond caress with which Maggie greeted her.

"Who would think of your breaking all one's bones in that way," she said, who loved so to have her bones broken.

"I had to break some body's!" was Maggie's answer, "I am so happy."

At the dinner table Aunt Jane proposed to go into the form of pairing Tom and Maggie, Horace and Annie together, but Horace said he should sit by his wife on his wedding day, and Annie, after upbraiding him for his want of chivalry to her, enchanted Tom by declaring that he alone should be at her side. She was in great spirits to-night, and felt it within her that she could entertain them all the whole evening if she chose to give herself the reins. But she was trying to keep a little check on her reckless tongue, and this gave the others a chance to speak, and to feel that a vivifying glow from Maggie was warming and cheering the whole circle.

"What has got into you, Maggie?" she whispered, in the course of the evening. "Have you heard some good news?"

"Why, I am just as usual," was the reply.

The mark on her forehead, the divine mark, was growing deeper, but she wist it not.

"I am coming to have a frolic with baby to-morrow," she added.

"Have you decided what to call her?" asked Aunt Jane.

"No, we haven't. Tom calls her Blanche, for a little sister he had once; think what an odd combination, Blanche White! And I call her Mag. I suppose she'll get one or the other of these names; probably the first.

"Annie, do be sober for one minute," cried Maggie, laughing. "You really never meant to have her called 'Mag?'"

"Why not? It's a nice name, and I have nice associations with it."

"You'll never let her do such a foolish thing, I know, Tom," said Maggie.

Tom smiled and looked wise. He knew what he was going to do when the last moment came, and he wished it had come. After dinner the two gentlemen withdrew from the society of the ladies, after the manner of men, and the three ladies got close together, after the manner of women thus slighted. Maggie had stumbled on a very interesting family connected with the Mission, and had a long story to tell about them, which she knew would result in a raid on Aunt Jane's store-closet next day.

"I wish I had time to run after poor folks as

you do," said Annie, "for you really seem to enjoy it. And Horace has beaten it into my old Tom's head that for the mere pleasure of it, letting the question of duty go, it is good to live for other people rather than for yourself."

"As if you had not learned that lesson via baby !" said Aunt Jane.

"Via baby and mamma White," said Annie. "Yes, I really think I know a few little things I did not know when I was married. And as for Tom, you never saw a man so changed. I wish you could see the letters he writes to his mission boys; I am sure they are enough to melt hearts of stone. I cried over them myself. And the other night, just as he had come home all tired out, de-pending on a half hour with baby before she went to bed, a message came that one of those boys was badly scalded, and off he went without his dinner, without me, and without baby."

"Was the boy so seriously injured?" asked Aunt Jane.

"Yes, his life was in danger. Tom talked and prayed with him; think of it, my Tom getting down on his knees in a tenement house ! And it was rather embarrassing for him, for there were neighbors all standing around, and one of the little children was dusting him all the time with a wisp-broom !"

"I don't know which pleases me most, his visiting and praying with his sick boys, or your loving sympathy with him in it," said Aunt Jane.

"Nor I," said Maggie. "It seems to me that God hasn't left me a single thing to wish for. He has given me everything I want." The young men now drew near, and conversation became general, and Annie made some gay allusions to past times, when they had all gathered around this same fireside, playing at cross-purposes with each other. Horace, who had suffered of late with intolerable sleepiness in the evening, and who had hardly been able to keep his eyes open since dinner, now roused up and answered her back, and they had an encounter of wits that greatly amused the rest of the company. When it was time for Annie to go, on account of that punctual and exacting little maiden at home, they all protested against her breaking in upon the evening so early. For, while to a looker-on they might have seemed a very quiet little company, they had been spending very happy hours together; one love and one hope drew them to each other; they were fellow-travelers, all going the same way, and before long at the longest, they would all meet where they need not separate to go to different homes.

"We always have such a nice time when we come here!" said Annie, as she kissed Aunt Jane good-night. "Are you sure that you are not really our very own aunty?"

"I am sure that I am very own aunty to all four of you," she said, looking lovingly upon them.

"What, and are you my aunt, too?" cried Tom. "How very delightful!"

"It is good to go out, if only to find how good it is to be at home again," said Horace, as he and Maggie hovered over their own little fire half an hour later. "Ah, Maggie, how many such homes as ours there might be if there was only a little more common sense in the world."

"Suppose we turn into apostles, and go about preaching that doctrine," said Maggie, laughing at his earnestness.

"I wish we could. Perhaps, when our heads get as gray as Aunt Jane's, people will begin to attach some weight to what we say, and we can then preach our sermons."

"I am not going to wait for that. In fact, we are preaching now. Every body must see that we are as happy and contented as people can be in this world. I, for one, am growing stout on it."

"You are growing sleepy — growing stout on want of exercise," replied Maggie. "But that horse will come; he will come, I am sure, and renew your youth. It did me good to hear you and Annie banter each other so this evening, for you have been growing silent and heavy of late; something so unnatural in you."

"Yes; the visit really did me good. I shall be all right when your magic horse comes to give me my shaking up."

So they helped each over the fact that their evenings were getting to be mortifying to Horace because he could not keep awake, disappointing to Maggie because she thus lost his society.

And while they were thus engaged, Aunt Jane was writing a kind little note to Tom, to tell him how she rejoiced over and sympathized in the Christian work to which he was giving himself. She had long since formed the habit of finding it good to scatter little pleasures along the pathway of life when no opportunity for greater deeds presented itself, and so these words to Tom. She was astonished, when his answer came to her, at the surprise and delight it had given him. Her eyes moistened as she read his grateful, affectionate words, and she thanked God that her old, lonely life had still power to send a ray of golden light into other lives.

But a few days later Tom came to her, and said in his simple, honest way, "Aunt Jane, your note has puffed me up so, that I almost wish you had not written it."

She smiled a little, then she said: "We have all read of the wand of a certain king that turned to pure gold every object it touched. Now, every Christian has a wand which works just such, nay, greater miracles. Fénelon prayed that the successes of Louis XIV. might make him as humble as a great humiliation could. Now you and I, when we feel ourselves unduly exalted by flattery, or even by innocent, loving words, have only to say, 'Lord, turn this temptation into benediction; let the words that strive to make me abound, become, in thine hands, but a new abasement,' and there will be no 'puffing up,' you may depend upon it."

"It made me very happy. But then I caught myself thinking, 'Tom, there must be something uncommon about you if people can write to you in that way!' And then I felt mean that I had thought anything about it." He looked in her face like an ingenuous, very good boy, and she said:

"I don't see but you'll have to pray that you may get back to thinking yourself common again. We have all of us a great deal to learn on these points, but we must learn to bear praise and blame with equal equanimity. We shall, in this world, get most of the latter, but we need shrink from neither as long as both drive us to Christ."

11*

"Now, I'm glad you sent me that note, and glad I've had this talk with you, Aunt Jane. My mother has often said she wished you could get hold of me, and now you have."

"I shall keep hold, you may depend," she answered. "I am an old woman, and might be a very sorrowful one; but I am resolved not to be that while there is a single human heart in the world that mine can warm."

"You are warming a good many," he said. "It is really wonderful how you make us young folks love you."

"It is not I whom you love!" she answered. "It is the presence within me of your and my Friend. Let Him leave me for one moment, and all you would see left would be a weak, sinful, ignorant old woman."

He only half caught her thought, and yet it held him all the way down town, and came back to him later with singular power.

"Well, Mag," said Annie, the next time they met, "Tom has made up his mind to give your name to baby, and says he always meant to do it. Only he is for sentimentalizing over her, and calling her 'Pearl' and 'Pearlie.' For my part I shall call her Mag. Sha'n't I, my little Daisy, my Queen Margaret, my wee Maggie, my white Pearl, my own old Mag?" she cried, snatching her baby from Maggie's arms to cover it with kisses.

"You've got to pray for this baby as long as you live," she added, her bright face growing softer, more tender. "She's got a poor old stick for her mother, and you must be her saint; I'm afraid I never shall. There, take her; I'm tired of her already. I never did like to hold one of these squirming little things."

Maggie stretched out her motherly arms, and gathered her little namesake to her heart of hearts. And while she half sang, half whispered to it of the great world of tenderness she had to give it, Annie, with nimble and skillful fingers, manufactured for herself a bonnet that she knew Tom would say became her wondrously, and so it did.

"I am not running up milliner's bills for grandma White," she said. "Now, isn't that lovely? Well, guess what it cost. You won't? Well, it cost four cents."

"You absurd child!" cried Maggie.

"Are you talking to me or to the baby? You see now how lucky it was that I brought home so many odds and ends from Paris. I can go on making bonnets indefinitely for nothing at all. Maggie, dear, you need not think my head runs on nothing better."

"I don't think so. I know it runs on Tom and the baby and on yet better things."

"Yes it does. But I know I am not all taken up with those better things as you are. What is the reason? I want to be good. I try to cure myself- of my ways, but I can't. Do you know what a trial I am to Tom's mother?"

"A trial? What, when you make Tom so happy, and have given her this sweet baby to love?"

"Well, I am a trial for all that. She has set you up for her standard and wants me to be just like you. Now I'll leave it to you if nature did not make us entirely different?"

"I can testify that she did," said Maggie, absorbed in the baby. And then, rousing herself, for she was trying to carry her unselfishness into very little things, she added,—

"Somebody has said that we ought to learn to love our friends for what they are, rather than for what we wish them to be. I think so too. But I must say that I never had to learn that in regard to you. You are lovable in yourself, and you know it, you naughty little thing you, with your mock-humility speeches."

"So is everybody," objected Annie, "if you can only get at the lovable part. The trouble is they keep their hearts locked up as they do their cash, and you only know they have any by seeing the boxes."

Maggie laughed. "But do not you and Tom's mother get on well together?"

"Oh, we get on; that's just the phrase to describe it! You know, in the first place, she's weak and nervous."

"And you are strong and well. So you can inspirit and cheer her."

"Well, I do. In the second place, she thinks she knows how to manage baby ten times as well as I do. She wants her bathed in hot water, and I bathe her in cold. She thinks she ought to have everything she cares for, and I think she shouldn't have one. She gives her great lumps of sugar, too, just think of that!"

"Still you have the chief control of baby, and always these little differences occur when there are grandmas on hand. It is not peculiar to you."

"You would not like it. You are as independent and as positive as I am, every bit of it."

"No, I should not like it. But I don't expect to find anything in this world exactly to my mind. I expect to plague people and expect them to plague me. But I would not make myself unhappy about such trifles if I had such a baby as this."

"Would you really like to have the baby and let grandma be thrown in."

"Would I?" cried Maggie. "Oh, Annie."

"I had no idea you felt so," said Annie, greatly

moved by Maggie's look and tone, and the clasp
of her arms around the little one. "I don't see,
then, why God does not give you children, if you
want them so much."

"Hush, dear, it hurts me to hear you so much
as hint that He is not giving me all it is best I
should have, for He is."

"Dear old Mag! I wish I loved Him as you do!
And I wish I could learn to mind little frictions
less. But it will take me a long, long time to get
back to where I was when worldly prosperity turned my giddy head. Tom is really better than I am;
it quite frightens me to see how fast he grows in
goodness. You ought to see the lovely note Aunt
Jane wrote him. Let me think, where is it? Oh,
here it is, read it, Maggie."

"Do you think I may?"

"Certainly. It is only some of those kind, en-
couraging words she loves to put on paper."

Maggie read the note with a keen appreciation
of the Christian love that prompted it, that could
only be felt by a kindred soul.

"It is beautiful," she said, "and just like Aunt
Jane. She lives for everybody except herself. Now
we are always going to her with all our little troubles, yet she never speaks of hers? But, of course,
she must have them as well as her great sorrows."

"I cannot associate the idea of trouble and sorrow with Aunt Jane," said Annie. "I never saw a cloud on her face."

"But she has them on her heart. Only shallow people are always at ease there. But she is cheerful because she will be cheerful. She is a constant lesson to me."

"To you! what is she, then, to me with all my little frets and cares?"

"A nice book to study!" replied Maggie. "I believe I shall take this baby home with me. You wouldn't care much!"

"Shouldn't I? Come here, little Mag, and tell your Aunt Mag some of your and my nice wee secrets."

How pretty she looked, this bright, rosy young mother, as she caught her child and whispered some loving nonsense in its ear! At least Maggie thought so as she walked home with a warm sisterly glow in her heart.

"Annie is going to make a splendid woman," she said to herself. "The worst of her is over, she will grow less and less selfish, more and more loving, every day. That baby will bring her out, I know it will."

Dear Maggie, it is you who will bring her out. But you will never know it. Walking down a fashionable avenue towards her obscure little home in a dress that befitted her poverty, but was out of keeping with that of the gay crowd about her, she had thoughts in her heart that made a "thousand liveried angels lacquey her," for they were thoughts such as angels love.

CHAPTER XIX.

WELL, my little wife, how has the day gone with you?" Horace asked, as she ran to meet him in the hall, on his return that night.

"It has gone well, like all my days," she said, gayly.

"So has mine, unlike all my days," he returned "I have something to tell you that will please you, I know."

"I hope it is about a horse."

"No; it is about a boy. About young Rooney. He has come out such a fair and square Christian. You know how he has tried my faith and patience. And only last Sunday he was so outrageous that if it had not been for my certainty that you were praying for him, I would have dismissed him from the school. But l resolved to give him one more chance, and to-day he came down to the office, to ask my pardon, and you never saw a fellow more humble and penitent. He says that his behavior on Sunday was the devil's parting grip, and that he has since then 'given him as good as he sent.' "

" What talk !"

" Oh, there's no cant or humbug about him, and there never will be. If he goes on he'll make an original, useful man."

" Yes, there's nobody like him."

" I wish you would be a little more enthusiastic, Maggie. I thought you would be perfectly delighted with this news."

" So I am. But you know I never can say anything when I feel greatly moved."

" Yes, I do know it. But I wish you would outgrow that. It makes people misunderstand you so."

" I suppose it does. But one must get used to being misunderstood. Tell me some more about Rooney ; it does my heart good."

" I will, after dinner. Oh, no ; after dinner I have to go and see Aunt Jane. I received a mysterious note from her this morning that I can make nothing of. Just run it over, and see if you can guess what she means."

Maggie turned pale, as she cast her eye over the note.

" Why, what can have happened to her since our visit ? She seemed then as well as usual, don't you think so ?"

" I saw no change in her except that, if that were possible, she seemed more delightful than ever. But it is plain that something is stirring her soul."

" Something very serious," said Maggie. " Do go, the moment dinner is over."

A shadow had fallen upon them both. Horace loved Aunt Jane with ever increasing devotion, and her love to him was one of the bright spots of his life. And Maggie loved her, not simply from gratitude, but with that wondrous Christian affection known to those only who are walking heavenward hand in hand.

Horace was gone all the evening. Maggie sat watching for him hour after hour, the passing footsteps were heard less frequently ; at last all was silence in the street, and still he came not. Could anything have happened to him ? she asked herself, with a pang. And supposing there had—what then ? Why, then—ah, who that saw that upturned face could have helped loving our Maggie !

" Are you all tired out waiting for your old husband ?" asked his welcome voice at last.

" Not tired now you have come !" she said, joyfully.

" Well, what is it, dear, good news or bad ?"

" Everything has two sides," he answered, evasively. " Aunt Jane will tell you, the next time you see her. But she has forbidden my doing it."

" I shall see her to-morrow, then."

" Yes.   You had better go."

She watched his face as he spoke, but could learn nothing from it, but she felt that his arms enfolded her more closely than usual, as if afraid she might slip away unawares.   But when, the next morning, she was ushered into Aunt Jane's bright parlor, and met her bright smile, she reproved herself for foolish anxieties.

" I don't think I shall let you give me such a hug as you did the other night," said Aunt Jane, holding her off a little, as she welcomed her. " Take off your things, darling, and we'll have a nice long talk.   I knew you were on the way here, knew at just about what hour you would come ; you know 'mind knows the approach of mind,' sometimes, at least."

"Yes. Your note to Horace startled me a little."

" I meant it should.   Maggie, dear, if I should tell you that I was about to go to Europe for some years, would it pain you very much ?"

" That depends on how glad you were to go. If you were glad, I am sure I should not be asking how I was to get along without you.   I should be thinking of your pleasure."

" Yes, you would.   Well, dear, don't be troubled then when I tell you that I am going on a much longer voyage, and shall not come back."

Maggie's color came and went, yet she did not say a word for some moments, but sat with the dear old hand clasped in both hers.

"Will the voyage be long? Will it be hard?" she whispered at last.

"Yes, dear; long and hard. But what then? Why, a beautiful getting into port, and the casting anchor there."

"Oh, Aunt Jane!"

"Do you know, my child, that I can look on curiously at your tears, and take no part in them? It seems such a very little thing for a woman of my age to drop down by the wayside. Why, it is happening every hour; why not to me?"

"And the suffering?"

"Oh, the flesh shrinks from that, of course. But still, what then? It is not the fashion of human souls to part company with the house of clay they have lived in without a hue and cry on the part of the latter. I suppose you have guessed my secret by this time?"

"Yes. And to think how I must have hurt you that night!"

"It did not signify. And now you will want to hear how long I have known this. I have known it six months. I may live six months more, but about that I have not inquired. All my worldly affairs, thanks to Horace, are now settled. But I

want the pleasure, before I go, of seeing you and
him more comfortably established. That house did
very well for a beginning, and you have both behaved beautifully in it. But I am a sort of mother
to you, you know, and I am going to beguile myself of some of my weary days by putting you into
another. You see it would be impossible to live
in such close quarters if you had children."

"But we have not any."

"Not now. Yet they're coming. I am not going to make you rich, but I am going to lift the
burden you have borne so patiently. No, do not
say a word; the thing is settled, and has long been
settled in my mind. Hitherto you two have not
had the necessaries of life; I have just found that
out."

"Why, Aunt Jane! We have had them and
more, too."

"No; I got it out of Horace last night how
heavy and sleepy he is every evening, and how
often depressed and out of sorts, and all for want
of proper exercise. I really think you owed it to
me, who loves you so, to tell me he had been ordered to ride. But those hard days are over. He
is to begin to ride this very day. And as to you,
my precious little Maggie, you shall have something to make your domestic wheels go easier, and
something for your poor folks besides. So you see

my going off to be well and happy by and by, is to add to your health and happiness, too."

"We would rather have you, and go on living forever, just as we have done."

"I have no doubt of it. But you see that God has other plans for you. And now we'll talk about the place I am going to, if you feel like it."

"Oh, Aunt Jane! You are glad you are going to leave us!"

"Yes—that is, I am glad I am going where I am, though not glad to leave you. Think how easily I can go! No husband, no child to hold me back, you and Annie and Horace are all nicely settled, and happy; why, it is wonderful! And I have so long felt more at home *there* than I have here. Not that I would have you fancy that I have not been happy, very happy, among you all."

"You have been ready to go this long time, I know."

"Yes, I have. If I were going to Europe now, I should have quite a time of it, making my preparations. But for this voyage I have not a thing to do. It was all made for me long, long ago; such kind and thoughtful and loving preparation! All I shall have to do will be to step on board."

"And we shall be following after," said Maggie, drying her tears. "I am ashamed of myself for crying so. I ought to be congratulating you in-

stead of putting on this doleful face. Dear Aunt
Jane, I will not do it again. You are going to enjoy a great deal more than we are going to suffer,
and what if we do suffer? Yes, I am ashamed of
myself."

"Ah, I am too happy in the thought of going to
mind your crying a little. I always was a selfish
old thing. But all that will soon be over. I shall
not be selfish in heaven. I shall never crimson
with shame or sigh with grief; I shall be with my
Saviour and like Him. All the rest of the time I
am here I want to spend in magnifying Him : but
I am afraid that towards the last I shall only be
able to do that in a very imperfect way. Remember, dear Maggie, youth and health are the time
and the season for glorifying Him. I am afraid a
sick bed, with its distracting pains and weaknesses,
is a poor place for it."

"I think you have glorified Him all along."

"Not as I now wish I had. Life looks very
strange and impressive as one casts on it a back-
ward glance. Perhaps you fancy that it looks insignificant. But it does not. On the contrary,
even its little details have an importance of their
own ; just as moments make hours, so trifles make
life ; not one can be spared out of the great whole,
each has its own account to give to God. And
now, dear, we'll make it a point, you and I, to have

very cheery meetings together, while I stay ; shall we not ?"

" I shall want to come very often, and I will be cheerful, too. This has been a great shock to me ; I want to get home and pray it over."

" Why can't we pray it over now ? For my part, I have on my soul such a weight of gratitude that I want to pray and sing, too. To think that I, a poor sinner, am so soon to be called home ! I can hardly believe it."

Maggie went home, after a time, with a full heart; fuller of joy than of pain, for the courage and faith of the one heart had strengthened and elevated the other. She found Annie waiting for her.

" I have been here an age," was her salutation. " But you have been crying. Why, Maggie, darling !"

" Yes, but I am ashamed of myself. Yet you will cry, too, when you hear about Aunt Jane."

She told the story in a few words, and Annie was, for a time, completely overcome with grief.

" Aunt Jane is just the same as an own aunt," she said, at last. " How dreadful it is to love people so ! Sometimes I wish I were as heartless as a stone. And you say she is bright and cheerful as ever ? Then she must have been inwardly sad and sorrowful when we thought her so happy. For, of course, it is the expectation of meeting her

12

husband and child again that makes her glad to die."

"Oh, I do not think so! She never mentioned them."

"I am sure that if Tom and baby should die, I should want to go too," pursued Annie.

Maggie knew that it would be of no use to argue this question. Annie was too far behind her in the Christian life to comprehend what she and Aunt Jane so well understood : that heaven is Christ, that Christ is heaven ; that that city hath no need of sun, or moon, or human food, or earthly tie, because the Lord Himself doth lighten it.

"I suppose I shall have to go to see her?" Annie asked, finding Maggie's silence not agreeable. "But I shall not know what to say to her. Do you think I need say anything? Wouldn't it do to talk of other things, and not of this?"

"You will not find it embarrassing at all. She will talk about dying just as honestly and naturally as she does about living. I would go to-day, if I were you."

"Oh, I can't go to-day—I've made such a fright of myself, crying. Perhaps I'll make Tom take me some evening. Dear me, how dreadful it all is!"

"You won't feel so after you've seen her. Think now, she has known it for six months, and not one of us has seen the least difference in her."

Yet Annie felt the dread and the repugnance to seeing Aunt Jane, that is natural enough in young people, and she put off from day to day the visit she yet felt she ought to make. So she was not a little ashamed when, one morning, Aunt Jame came to see her.

"As the mountain wouldn't come to Mahomet, Mahomet has had to come to the mountain," was the salutation that greeted her as she entered the parlor. "You need not be afraid of your old aunt because she is on the wing."

"Oh, Aunt Jane, I was so shocked, so grieved!"

"Shocked that I have had an invitation from a King? Grieved that I am going to accept it joyfully? Why, my child, the past six months have been delightful ones!"

"You must have loved your husband and your son with wonderful love," said Annie.

"My husband, my son? Aye, and so I did. But it is not to find them that I am going on this long, hard journey; though I doubt not I shall find them at its ending. Listen to me, and never forget my words. I loved my husband and my boy with a mad idolatry that made heaven, when they went there, only heaven because it had become their home. And now I love Christ so that heaven is only heaven because it is His eternal abode. Don't you remember, dear, how you children, when you

had been away at school, always asked, on your return, ' Is mother at home ?' never adding, ' and father and all the rest of them.'   And if mother was
at home you were satisfied, even if the others were
all absent, and came in later."

Annie listened, but with a troubled face. " No
one can make me believe," she said, at last, with
great decision, "that I could be contented in heav-
en without Tom and baby."

Would it have done any good to argue the point
with her ? Suppose a child of four years says to
his mother, " I am as tall now as I ever shall be,"
can she prove to his faithless, ignorant little mind,
that this is not true ? No ; she can only say,
" Wait, and see !"

But Annie wanted to dispute and argue, and
kept trying to lead Aunt Jane into a discussion.
" It stands to reason," she said, "that if I could not
be happy without them here, I could not there.
For I have God for my Friend now ; and yet I want
my husband and baby, besides. Why did he give
them to me? Was it not that I might love them ?"

But as Aunt Jane only smiled kindly at her ve-
hement, excited words, Annie checked herself, and
came back to the point whence she had started,
and said how dreadful it all was.

" There is nothing dreadful about it yet, dear,
and when that part of it comes you will be away

in the country with your baby, and need see none of it."

"Ah, but you will suffer, all the same."

"Yes, I know. But I shall forget all that when I've been in heaven five minutes."

"And you really want to die?"

"It is not so much wanting to die as to live. For once out of this world my real life will begin. That thought makes me very happy."

"I don't want to go till Tom and baby do," said Annie, returning uneasily to that thought. "It wouldn't be heaven if they were not there."

We are only too apt to yield to the self-conceit, beloved child of ignorance, that utters such cries. It would be well if we could once get it into our heads that those who express religious views to which we are strangers, have gained them, as he who travels in advance of his comrade sees, before he does, what there is to be seen on the way. And instead of arguing with him who spies out the land, and brings back grapes from Eshcol, suppose we penetrate that land, and look for the fruit it has likewise in store for us.

> "Hast Thou but one blessing, O my Father?
> Bless me, even me also!"

Aunt Jane was like a mariner, who, foreseeing a coming storm, trims his sails, and, if need be, casts

overboard his treasures. She knew that all her
faith and patience, and natural courage, were now
about to be tested, and that good people and bad
people would look to see how she met the gale.
But before it broke loose upon her in relentless
fury, she busied herself with the interests of all
those who would be in any way affected by her
death. She determined to see with her own eyes
that the burden was lifted from some of the homes
she loved. Naturally enough, she thought first of
Horace and Maggie. She did not propose to make
them rich, but only to make their way easier. And
the plan of putting them into a more comfortable
house, grew out of their grief at the thought of
parting with her. She thought that moving and
getting into their new abode would be a wholesome distraction for them, and that when her hard
struggle came, there would be full time for them
to weep and mourn. She had great sympathy,
too, for country ministers and their wives, and had
not a few on her heart to whom she now gave a
loving, helping hand. Then when those affairs
were all arranged, there was an endless number of
little blessings to scatter here and there; parting
visits to make, while possessing her secret, and so
avoiding a formal farewell; letters to write, kind
words to speak, sick rooms to beautify. She
thought of everything and everybody, and kept on

the wing long after many a less courageous sufferer would have fainted and fallen. And now she was so full of love and sympathy that she turned not a few heads; not knowing out of what a storehouse she gave to them, each fancied himself a peculiarly favored hero, and went about rich and happy in gems of affectionate words that she flung about with lavish hands, as we throw pebbles. If her spirits flagged, if at times she said to herself, "This cannot, must not be," no eye witnessed the conflict; she fought her battles in silence and in prayer and won her victories there also.

Neither Horace nor Maggie took much pleasure in their new home, though they knew the change was good in every respect. But to Horace, Aunt Jane was little less than a mother; he loved her only less than he loved his wife, and the thought of seeing her suffer, and then of parting with her, at times overwhelmed him. And Maggie, in addition to the love she naturally felt for her, knew that there was a wonderfully golden link between them; the love stronger than death, that unites together those who have perfect Christian sympathy. Her counsellor, her guiding star, was about to be taken from her, and how many a long year might pass before they should meet again! But such shadows are good for us, and perpetual sunshine is not These twain clung together, and clung to Christ as prosperity could not have made them do; they were sad and sorrowful, but not gloomy or unhappy. The thorny path bears some of the sweetest flowers that adorn life; and when with naked, bleeding feet we walk upon a flinty soil, we often find diamonds. But nobody believes that save those who have dared the thorn and the flint, plucked the flower, and seized the gem.

"It really does my heart good," said Aunt Jane, lying back in her chair and looking about her, "to see how much more comfortable you and Horace are in this house than you were in the other There'll be frolicking on these wide stairs one of these days, you may depend. And how much better Horace seems."

"You have been too good to us, Aunt Jane," was Maggie's answer. "But, then, you always were."

"You mean that God has been too good to me. And so He has. Well, I am very glad to see you in your new home before I go to mine."

"You have been like a mother to a great many young people, as well as to us. What makes you so fond of us? I thought that as people grew old they lost sympathy with those who had less experience of life, and only enjoyed the society of the very wise and the very good," said Horace.

"Ah, but I never grew old! I often tried to do so, but I couldn't. You young creatures, with your little romances, your honeymoons, your smiles and your tears, kept me always on the *qui-vive*. And now I wish I could tell you how easy I feel about leaving you. I see you so happy in each other, so happy in God and in working for Him, that I have not a wish ungratified. You will have your trials and your sorrows, your rainy days and your tempestuous ones; and what is worse, you will have your prosperous ones. But you will not be overwhelmed by the one or swept away by the other."

"You will give us ever so much good counsel before you go, won't you, dear Auntie?" asked Maggie, tearfully.

"Good counsel! ah, it is easily given. It is this: *Take counsel of God*. Everything I have to say is included in that."

They were all silent for a long time after this. Yet it was not the silence that separates, but that which unites. Aunt Jane lay back again in her chair, looking pale and exhausted, but there was a smile on her lips, and her bright eyes seemed to penetrate into a far future, into ineffable peace and joy.

"To think," she said, at last, "that I am really on the wing! Half way there!"

12*

They sat on each side, holding one of her hands in theirs, and could almost see what she saw.

"This is my first and last visit in this house of yours, my children," she said, when it was time to take leave. "That is to say, it is the last I shall make in this old tumble-down of a body. But I shall often be here in spirit, watching you and blessing you, if I may."

"Shall we know it?" whispered Maggie.

"I fancy not. But I see no reason why departed friends should not hover over beloved ones still upon earth, watching their progress and rejoicing in it."

"But all their friends will not be making progress," said Horace.

"Perhaps that painful sight will be hidden. However, it is all speculation. And now, dear children, I must go. Peace be within these walls!"

She drove home in silence, though Horace was with her, for she was extremely fatigued. A faithful, dearly loved servant came to meet her as she reached her own door.

"That's right, Sarah. I knew you would be waiting. Before long it will be my turn to be waiting and watching for you. Good night, Horace, my own dear boy."

There was nothing new in these words, but they fell painfully on his ear. Yes, he was her boy, her dear boy, her own dear boy. She had done more towards making and saving him than any other human being. How many times in his thoughtless youth her prayers had so hedged him round that he could not get out! How many times they had called to the rescue that blessed Spirit that is ever waiting to be gracious, yet waits to be called. He would have been glad to throw himself into her arms and cry like a child, but no one should ever do that any more.

So he went sorrowfully away to his home, and he and Maggie wept and prayed there. And Aunt Jane entered hers to leave it no more. She had come to the very limit of her strength, and now, exhausted in body, but with an undaunted soul, she retired from the gaze of the world to fight a battle whose terrible scenes have found no record, save in a few faithful hearts that witnessed and shared them. It was a battle, but ever and anon she stopped to bind up the wounds of a fellow sufferer; now there was a quaint word that made her tearful watchers smile in spite of themselves; now there was a hymn, and now a song, and now a shout of victory.

"Oh, Aunt Jane! will this never be over?" Maggie asked, when months came and went and came, and only brought new pain, more weariness. "How can I see you suffer so another day?"

"Don't tell God that. For once let Him have His own way. Think of the end, darling."

"And mayn't I ask Him to let you go?"

"You may ask Him"—with a smile—"but He will listen to me, not to you. He won't dismiss me till school is done, nor would I go till then."

But only a few days later "school was done;" the bright-eyed, faithful scholar went home.

CHAPTER XX.

AMONG those who stood around that dying bed, Horace and Maggie were wanting. For there was a little life waking just as the pilgrim life was ending, and that life belonged to them. Aunt Jane and the infant who brought joy to sorrow "met upon the threshold, going out and coming in." What strange sport of nature was this?

> "Going out unto the triumph, coming in unto the fight;
> Coming in unto the darkness, going out unto the light."

Nay, what a wondrous choice it was of the Will that rules every destiny and arranges the exact moment for all comings and goings!

"They met upon the threshold." Did they recognize each other? Did the parting pilgrim hastily snatch from her shoulders the mantle she needed no more, and enfold in it the child she would have felt to be almost her own?

Did the little one as he passed her hear the rustle of no angelic wings? Who knows what mysterious communion took place upon that threshold, or will learn the secrets of the soul that went and the soul that came?

Sorrow and joy contended together in the two hearts where Aunt Jane's memory was enshrined. Their wondrous delight in their child needed to be tempered and subdued, and God gave the long-delayed gift at a moment when joy tempered grief. So he was cradled in the sanctity of days of mourning, yet welcomed with smiles that chased away tears.

The boy was a marvel of beauty and of health; he was just like Horace and just like Maggie, and they were absolutely unlike in race, unlike in character.

"Well," said Annie, after a critical study of the young hero," "I thought there never was a baby like mine, but this fellow throws her right into the shade. I am envious and jealous and glad and proud all at once. I wish I were a man, so that he could be named for me. Can't you manage it somehow, Maggie, you old darling, you?"

The "old darling" only smiled a rapturous smile. She was too happy to talk. The baby seemed to her nothing less than a miracle, a wonderful creation, no copy of anything on earth, and to be copied by none.

As to Horace, he contrived to let every one of
his clients know within a week that he had entered
into possession of a wonderful piece of property,
whose value could not be rated by millions of gold.
How proud, how happy he was! And if sometimes amid his joy a secret voice whispered, "Oh
that Aunt Jane had lived to see him!" another
voice whispered, "She has."

"What a splendid little fellow, what a perfect
copy of you!" Horace said to Maggie on the day
his son and heir enchanted him by a smile of recognition. "This is the very smile you gave me
that day on the train. Do you remember?"

"Do I remember? Oh, Horace! But this is
your smile, not mine. I was saying so to Annie
not an hour ago, and she agreed with me."

"I always hoped he would be like you," Horace
went on. "I hope he won't have a particle of my
old Adam."

"He'll have plenty of his own without borrow-
ing yours. Do you know what my father says
about giving him his name? But of course you
don't, for his letter came after you went down
town. I did not know father was so romantic.
See, this is what he says:

"'Do not inflict the dismal name of Jeremiah
upon your happy little boy. Give him a name by
which his wife can call him.'"

" His wife !" cried Horace, greatly amused.

"I don't see anything to laugh at," said Maggie.
"You were a baby once yourself, and yet you got
married when your time came. Ain't you almost
sorry ?"

Everybody who has a heart knows what Horace
said as he clasped his wife and his boy to his breast,
and thanked God for them both.

"I have been wishing that we could name him
for Aunt Jane," said Maggie at last. "It was she
who took such pains with me, taught me all I
know, loved me so much better than I deserved,
and at last gave me to you. I owe everything to
her, everything."

"And I owe more than everything. Yes, our boy
shall have her name, and if his little wife—do you
suppose he has one on earth ?—doesn't like it better
than Jeremiah, why she shan't be his little wife."

So the baby was baptized Faulkner, but did not
care in the least, and instead of screaming through
the ceremony, laughed and crowed and made himself very much at home, winning smiles and winning friends by the score.

"You see how it is, Mag," said Annie, afterwards, commenting on the scene, "you may be
ever so good yourself, but your children will act
just like other peoples'."

"Why shouldn't they ?" asked Maggie.

Whereat Annie smiled mysteriously, and flew home to her own little Mag, a quaint, wee morsel of a maiden, who, tiny as she was, ruled grandma with a rod of iron and was spoiled by papa.

And Maggie's little lordly visitant had everything his own way and carried all before him for a time. But, to his great surprise and displeasure, there came a day when he found that his young mother loved him so dearly that she was determined to have his perfect obedience, cost what it might. They had their little conflicts and shed their tears, but always came forth from every little battle better friends than ever, and Horace, busy all day in his office, and witnessing none of these encounters, believed that his boy was an exception to all rules and was born all docility, as he was all energy and life and fire.

Meanwhile Maggie was trying, while faithful to her child, to resume her old life and work for everybody, share everybody's joys and sorrows, and train her Mission girls for usefulness and happiness. It was hard work, but she managed it, just as people always manage to do what they choose. Only she could not go to seek work, but let it come to her, as it always will come to loving hearts and busy hands.

It had long been a favorite wish of Horace to make his house a home to young men who were living as he had lived, homeless and wifeless, and he could now indulge this wish, since he was not confined to a mere box. And he had only to open his hospitable doors, there were any number of friendless waifs who found no fireside so cheery, no home so attractive as his.

On one of these evenings, when Maggie had skipped up-stairs to her baby, feeling not much older than he did, Frank Ray, one of these waifs, took occasion to open his mouth on this wise:

"Seeing you and your wife so happy together in this pleasant home makes a fellow a little envious and a little restless. I suppose you know all about such feelings."

"Yes, and I went straightway and married a wife," was the reply.

"But what is a man to do whose tastes are domestic and simple, in love withal, but who is too poor to marry? And you know this city is full of such men."

"He is to do what I did. Bring down his notions to the level of his purse, and get married."

"But has a poor man a right to ask a young lady living at ease in her father's house to come down to the level of homely poverty?"

"Other things being equal, he is wiser if he selects a young lady who has been accustomed to the cares and annoyances inseparable from strait-

ened means.   But if he happens to fall in love with
one in a different sphere, of course, his position is
somewhat embarrassing.   Yet, if his love is returned, if he has really met his fate, I do not see
why he should not ask her to share his poverty.
for my part, I should want a woman to marry me
for love, not for the ordinary luxuries a man without a heart could give her."

"But see how 'the girl of the period' dresses!"

"I wouldn't marry a girl of the period."

"A man must be pretty wise in his own conceit,
who, being poor, fancies he can catch and tame
one of these glittering creatures.   But you must
allow that there are all degrees and types of this
girl.   I have in my mind one who is modest, amia-
ble, and refined; she dresses richly, but not ex-
travagantly, not showily.   I have loved her in secret five years.   And I have not the smallest *reason*
to think she prefers me to half a dozen other
young men who hover round her.   Yet, love does
not care for reason, but *feels its way*."

"Yes; and there comes a time when it must
speak out, or die."

"Well, I have got to just that point, and stand
trembling on the brink of my fate.   If I could
offer her a comfortable home I would not wait
another day.   But to ask her to leave all those
luxuries for my pleasure!"

"Ah! there's just where you make a grand mistake. What luxury can feed and satisfy an empty heart? For aught you know, hers is starving in the midst of plenty. And what luxury born of money can compare with that of loving and being beloved?"

Frank Ray's face was a study for its rapture. But he soon subsided.

"She refused a man who loved her passionately," he said.

Horace shrugged his shoulders.

"Now, you are misjudging her!" cried Frank. "You fancy she ran and told of it, and so it got round to me. It is no such thing. He told me the whole story himself, and her part in it elevated her in my eyes, as it did in his. She asked him if she had ever given him encouragement by look, word, or tone; he owned that she had not. She said she had long seen, with pain, his attachment to her, and had *conscientiously and persistently* concealed her real liking for him, in order to spare him the mortification she was now giving him. She went on to say that it cost real self-denial to treat with coldness and indifference a man whom she would have delighted to treat as a highly-prized, intimate friend. 'Why should it not?' she asked. 'Women are as susceptible to friendship as to love.' She appeared so doubly charming in this interview, showed so much real feeling for him, and such real nobility of character, that he made another frantic appeal to her heart."

"Very silly—very wrong!" Horace put in.

"Do you think so?"

"Yes! What right had he to pursue and distress her in that way? Surely, such a young lady as you describe her to be knew her own mind."

"She did. But in his excitement and pain he thought of himself only, and let drop a word about his poverty, that she caught up with an indignation that dried her tears, declaring that men little knew the hearts of women, if they fancied they needed the bribe of wealth."

"Good!" ejaculated Horace. "I advise you to try your chance with her by all means."

"But she has never given me the right. Through all these years, when she must have seen my attachment, she has never spoken a word or looked a look that gave encouragement. She very rarely will go out with me, never wrote me a scrap of a note, though I have contrived excuses for writing dozens to her, never lent me a book, or advised me to read one. Now, can there be real heart concealed behind all this propriety? If she cared for me, would not there be a chance betrayal, a glance of joy in the eye when we met?"

"Oh, they're incomprehensible creatures, all of

them. And you intimated that you had some hope."

"It is the hope of a fool, or a madman," returned Frank. "But I ought not to trespass thus on your time. Indeed, I do not know how I came to open my mind to you at all."

"This little Paradise of mine has been the means of opening not a few hearts to me and my wife," Horace replied, with some just pride. "Those who have got into the heart of this happy home have wanted to know its secret, seeing plainly that money had little to do with it; and as you have confided in me, I will be equally frank with you, and tell you this secret in a few words—we love God, and we love each other!"

"It shall not be my fault if there is not a home just like it!" was the reply.

And it turned out that there was a girl in the period, if not of it, who was capable of recognizing a loyal and loving heart when she met it, and of doing without some of the little outside advantages its possessor could not offer. She left a home where she had everything she wanted, except just what she gained in leaving it; she entered a home where she had to do without style and elegance, and put up with the faithful affection of a good man. The first time we meet her let us congratulate her.

And now we have come to the fifth anniversary of the marriages that have beguiled us of not a few hours, and we see Horace and Maggie for the last time. Horace sits with his boy on his knee, and his wife by his side, the picture of a satisfied, happy man. Tom and Annie are on the other side of the fire, with little May, and there is a new light and a new grace on Annie's face, for she is not thinking of herself, but of the fairy figure in her arms, on which she looks with a fondness that her first-born child never called forth. For Annie is of the sort to be ever growing; to be ever ripening, ever becoming more meet for this world, more akin to the harmonies of the next. But let her grow and ripen as she will; let her become wise, and good, and unselfish, and loving, only one pair of eyes will ever see in her the tender, womanly, Christian grace that shines in the face and breathes in the atmosphere of "our Maggie!"

But here Adam Jr., declares, "I thought I had verily found a guide to matrimony in these pages, and should soon find myself in the Garden of Eden. But here I am out in the cold, with nothing left me but a commonplace photograph of two husbands, two wives, a boy, a girl, and a baby!"

But, Adam Jr., guide-books do not pretend to do your traveling for you. They leave you a free agent, and offer statistics rather than advice. If

you wish to enter the Garden of Eden, why don't
you do it? You cannot afford it? If that is literally true, you will have to wait in patience till you
can. This will have the effect to make you far
more worthy of your little Eve than you are now;
you will be growing wiser, more moderate, every
day, and richer in self-control; for an Almighty
hand shapes your destiny, and sees that your hour
has not yet come. But you can afford it, yet cannot find a Saint Margaret, or a Bird of Paradise,
and are not sure you fancy those particular types
of character? Yes! but she who was born into
this world to be your special choice and future joy
lives somewhere in it, and will come to you, or
you will go to her, at just the right moment.
Meanwhile, what do you want of her? To love
you, to guide your house, to bear your children,
to put up with all your faults and foibles, to merge
her individuality in yours, and, self-forgetting, be
by you forgot? Then no Garden of Eden opens
before you, and you shall live in a land full of
thorns and thistles.

Seek rather one whom you will love, honor, and
cherish, in spite of her human weaknesses; whom
you will ever allow to be herself, and to whom
you shall render an absolutely unselfish devotion.
Marrying on such terms, you will find her, whatever her natural character, vying with you to see

which shall do most loving, honoring, and cherish-
ing; which shall be most ready, not merely to live,
but to let live; which shall be most purely unselfish
and devoted. She cannot walk side by side with
a man of true nobility of character without becoming herself elevated and ennobled.

But she has not come to you, and you would
fain know where to seek her? Well, we do not
gather grapes of thorns, or figs of thistles, and we
do find rose-buds where we see full-blown roses.
It is a rash experiment to make an Eve of a maiden
who was born of a frivolous, selfish mother; and a
pretty safe one to pluck a bud from a bush that
you know to be a genuine rose tree. To be sure,
this matured, matronly woman, who is your ideal
of what is truest and best in her sex, has not become such by accident, and if you find her daughter crude and far below her in moral worth, remind yourself of the years of discipline that have
rounded out, mellowed, and perfected this character. She has had her crying babies, and her provoking servants, and all the little trials inseparable
from domestic life; she has grown unselfish and
loving by slow and painful degrees; if you would
fain marry her, in spite of her age, and because of
her virtues, she would not have you, for her heart
still belongs to him whose name she bears. No,
you are crude and immature yourself, and so is

13

your Eve; you must grow good, as you do old, *together!*

"But," you whisper, "I have found a wife, and married. I love her, she loves me, but we do not live in Paradise. She has little ways that at times make me desperate; and she declares that I have mine, which are as greatly repugnant to her."

"Of course! She fancied, when you told her she was an idol, at whose shrine you should ever worship, that you spoke the truth. But you meant just the reverse, while, perhaps, unconscious of the fact. You intended to sit on a pedestal and let her worship you; and she is inclined to do it, and would if she could. But then there are 'your ways!' Well, what are they? Let us ask Eve herself, since you won't confess."

"In the first place, he smokes; and he knows I hate smoke. How *can* men want to make themselves so disagreeable! Then he always, if a point is under discussion, makes me yield. And he often speaks to me in such a fault-finding, displeased way, that I cry my eyes out as soon as he leaves the house."

What! you leave the house with harsh words on your lips that will rankle in a heart that, whatever its weaknesses, loves you, and would gladly love more if you would make yourself worthy of it? Take the next up-town stage, go home, and tell her you are ashamed of yourself, kiss away her tears, and tell her that you never will part from her in anger again. And you are wilful, and never give way to her? You smoke, though it makes her sick? Ah, no wonder you do not live in Paradise! You will have to get down on your knees and pray that the root and ground of all your domestic failures may be done away with, that love to God may take the place of the love of self, and that you may learn the wholesome lesson of forbearance and gentleness, which He alone can teach.

But you say that Eve chafes your temper by always being behind hand; that she is not a nice housekeeper, that she spoils your children, that she spends too much money.

Now, then, Eve, it is your turn. It is your Christian duty to learn punctuality and precision. If it annoys Adam, Jr., to find dust on his table or his books, it is your duty to see that no dust settles there. If you have his food prepared and served in a slovenly way, it is high time to turn over a new leaf. If you are spoiling his children by foolish indulgence, cease from that perilous course at once. And remember that reckless expenditure is little less than wilful theft.

You cannot thus revolutionize your character and habits? True. But He who made you a wife and mother well understands all your difficulties, and is ready to remodel you the instant you are ready to permit Him to do it. But you reply that neither your husband nor yourself sustain any vital relation to Him; dare not take Him into your counsels; are not in the habit of looking to Him for sympathy or for help. Ah, now we come to the root of the matter! Your lives are hid, not with Christ in God, but in self, and it is hardly possible to conceive of any but a Christian marriage as being a very happy one. You may and do have your hours of delight in each other, but you have yet to learn the calm peace of those whose human frailties are daily giving way before the indwelling of a new life, that crowds out, roots out, *slays* the old selfish life.

There is many a little heaven here below; there is many a patient husband, many a true wife, ripening in these outskirts of Paradise for the Eden that is yet to come. Where is the man, where is the woman, who cannot help to form and happily dwell in such a home?

FINIS.

Recommended Other Reading
Available Through Calvary Press...

Stepping Heavenward
by Elizabeth Prentiss
Foreword by Elisabeth Elliot

New Deluxe Edition
includes "The History of the Book"
by George Prentiss

A nineteenth century Christian woman speaks to you through the ages in this timeless classic written in journal-style. Follow her as she takes you on a journey to spiritual maturity, from the age of sixteen—until just before her death. In the last century, over 200,000 women had their lives transformed by this wonderful work. Now this new, attractively bound edition will influence a whole new generation of readers. Buy a copy for a friend and share the experience. **Elisabeth Elliot** has called it "a treasure trove of godly and womanly wisdom." **Joni Eareckson Tada** states, "I can see how God will use it in a dramatic way in the lives of many women." "I highly recommend it!," says **Kay Arthur.**

ISBN 1-879737-29-9

call us toll-free!... **1-800-789-8175**

More Love To Thee
The Life and Letters
of Elizabeth Prentiss

by George Lewis Prentiss
Preface by Elisabeth Elliot

So many of our readers have sought to find this book, that Calvary Press felt a need to bring it back into print. In this biography and collection of letters, you are not only introduced to Elizabeth Prentiss, but through her husband's sweet recollections and her own words you begin to feel as if you know her personally. If *Stepping Heavenward* tugged on your heart, then get to know the dear Christian woman who penned it using aspects of her own life's experiences as the basis for much of the story. **Elisabeth Elliot** writes in her Preface. "Reading Christian biographies has had an immeasurable influence in my life and spiritual growth. *More Love To Thee* reveals the character of a woman who loved God and earnestly sought to help others to love Him."

ISBN 1-879737-14-0

visit our website!... calvarypress.com

The Little Preacher
Elizabeth Prentiss
Foreword by Elisabeth Elliot

Have you ever wondered how God forms a man's
character and prepares him to preach? Take a journey into the Black Forest of Germany as the author
of *Stepping Heavenward* shows us the experiences of
one poor family—and how the Lord's "Preacher
Preparation Program" works. Far from being a staid
treatise on the ministry, this book contains a story
that all ages will enjoy and treasure. A priceless gem,
Elisabeth Elliot states that "...the love of God per-
vades the story...a lovely book."

ISBN 1-879737-10-8

call us toll-free!... **1-800-789-8175**

Coming in 1999!...

Stepping Heavenward Audio Edition!
(complete and unabridged)

The Home at Greylock by Elizabeth Prentiss
Regarded as one of her finest works, it forms
the last book in the "trilogy" begun with
Stepping Heavenward and *Aunt Jane's Hero*.

**Contact us for more information
about these and our other titles!**

visit our website!... calvarypress.com

The Mission of Calvary Press

The ministry of Calvary Press is firmly committed to printing quality Christian literature relevant to the dire needs of the church and the world at the dawn of the 21st century. We unashamedly stand upon the foundation stones of the Reformation of the 16th century—Scripture alone, Faith alone, Grace alone, Christ alone, and God's Glory alone!

Our prayer for this ministry is found in two portions taken from the Psalms: "And let the beauty of the LORD our God be upon us, And establish the work of our hands for us; Yes, establish the work of our hands," and "Not unto us, O LORD, not unto us, but to Your name give glory" (Ps. 90:17; 115:1).

For a complete catalog of all our titles,
please be sure to call us at
1-800-789-8175
or visit our new website:
calvarypress.com